JESUS
& UTOPIA

JESUS & UTOPIA

✳✳✳

LOOKING

for the

KINGDOM *of* GOD

in the

ROMAN WORLD

✳✳✳

MARY ANN BEAVIS

FORTRESS PRESS
Minneapolis

JESUS AND UTOPIA
Looking for the Kingdom of God in the Roman World

Cover design: Brad Norr Design
Interior design: James Korsmo

Library of Congress Cataloging-in-Publication Data

Beavis, Mary Ann.
  Jesus and utopia : looking for the kingdom of God in the Roman world /
Mary Ann Beavis.
      p. cm.
  Includes bibliographical references and indexes.
  ISBN-13: 978–0–8006–3562–6 (alk. paper)
  ISBN-10: 0–8006–3562–0 (alk. paper)
  1. Christianity and politics. 2. Jesus Christ. 3. Kingdom of God. 4.
Jesus Christ—Kingdom. 5. Utopias. 6. Utopias—Religious
aspects—Christianity. I. Title.
  BR115.P7B34 2006
  270.1—dc22
                           2006020540

Manufactured in the U.S.A.
10   09   08   07   06   1   2   3   4   5   6   7   8   9   10

Contents

Abbreviations

1QS	*Community Rule* (Qumran Scroll)
2 En.	*2 Enoch*
11QMelch	*Melchizedek* (Quamran text)
ABD	*Anchor Bible Dictionary*, edited by David Noel Freedman, 6 vols. (New York: Doubleday, 1992)
Apoc. Ab.	*Apocalypse of Abraham*
Apoc. Mos.	*Apocalypse of Moses*
Apoc. Sedr.	*Apocalypse of Sedrach*
BDAG	Bauer, W., F. W. Danker, W. F. Arndt, and F. W. Gingrich, *Greek-English Lexicon of the New Testament and Other Early Christian Literature* (3rd ed.; Chicago: University of Chicago Press, 1999)
CBET	Contributions to Biblical Exegesis and Theology
DSS	Dead Sea Scrolls
HSM	Harvard Semitic Monographs
HTR	*Harvard Theological Review*
JSJ	*Journal for the Study of Judaism in the Persian, Hellenistic and Roman Periods*
JSNTSup	Journal for the Study of the New Testament: Supplement Series
JSOTSup	Journal for the Study of the Old Testament: Supplement Series

JSPSup	Journal for the Study of the Pseudepigrapha: Supplement Series
LCL	Loeb Classical Library
NRSV	New Revised Standard Version
Pss. Sol.	*Psalms of Solomon*
QM	*Milhamah* (War Scroll)
SNTSMS	Society for New Testament Studies Monograph Series
T. Ab.	*Testament of Abraham*
T. Dan.	*Testament of Daniel*
T. Mos.	*Testament of Moses*
War	Josephus, *Jewish War*

INTRODUCTION:
ANCIENT UTOPIAS, JESUS,
and the KINGDOM *of* GOD

Joseph of Arimathea, a respected member of the council, who was also himself waiting expectantly for the kingdom of God, went boldly to Pilate and asked for the body of Jesus.

—Mark 15:43; cf. Luke 23:51

Contemporary scholarship on the historical Jesus agrees that the announcement of the kingdom of God (*hē basileia tou theou*) was central to his teaching. However, the consensus that the kingdom played an important role in Jesus' ministry is not matched by agreement as to what the phrase meant to him and his circle. Mark 15:43 points to some of the challenges inherent in the interpretation of the phrase. Should the verb *prosdechomai* be translated, as it is in the NRSV, to mean that Joseph was "waiting for" or "expecting" the kingdom of God or that he "was accepting" it or "receiving it favorably"?[1] That is, did the evangelist mean to say that Joseph was looking for the kingdom's advent in the future or that he was already experiencing it? Does the assertion that he was "also" (*kai*) seeking the kingdom mean that he was a disciple of Jesus (as Matthew and John redact the verse; see Matt 27:57; John 19:38) or that he was part of a larger basileia movement sympathetic to Jesus? The question of the temporal reference to the kingdom, especially, is one of many that have occupied scholars for more than a century.

In an effort to contribute a new perspective to the discussion, this book will bring together two bodies of inquiry: the study of the kingdom of God in the teaching of Jesus, and the study of ancient utopian literature. Despite the patently utopian nature of Jesus' language of the kingdom—a realm ruled by God is bound to be "an ideal commonwealth where perfect justice and social harmony exist"[2] —this kind of investigation has not previously been undertaken. There are a few article-length studies of biblical and cognate utopias by biblical scholars,[3] and some utopian scholars have included the kingdom of God in their analyses of ancient utopias.[4] However, to date, no comprehensive consideration of the kingdom of God in ancient utopian context has appeared.

Of course, it was not until the sixteenth century that Sir Thomas More coined the term *utopia* in his book about an ideal, communistic society on a remote island.[5] The name of the island, Utopia, is a word-play on the Greek *ou-topos,* "no place" and *eu-topos,* "good place."[6] In the sixteenth and seventeenth centuries, the term was used to describe literary works modeled on More's *Utopia,* which "adhered more or less to traditional literary devices that More himself had received from Lucian of Samosata, who in turn had inherited them from Hellenistic novels, many of them no longer extant."[7] That is, although the word *utopia,* with its double meaning of "no place" and "good place," is not ancient, it would easily have been understood by ancient Greek-speaking audiences, and More's work was informed by classical and hellenistic accounts of ideal societies that were known to ancient authors, including hellenistic Jewish writers. In contemporary academic planning and architecture literature, the distinction is sometimes made between "utopia" as unattainable ideal and "eutopia" as activity that seeks the betterment of society: "to make the world a better place, to create supportive, and when possible, beautiful places and things for people."[8] In this study, this terminological distinction will be maintained, with *utopia* generally referring to imaginary ideal societies and *eutopia* referring to efforts or movements with the goal of improving society.

Due to its long, rich, and varied history, spanning a range of traditions from the ancient world to the present day, utopian thought is notoriously difficult to define. As E. D. S. Sullivan notes,

> For most people, the word "utopianism" has a popular connotation which has little to do with familiarity either with More or his book. . . . Over the intervening centuries, utopianism has taken on a significance of its own which includes, but goes far beyond, the condescending dictionary definition ("visionary or impractical") and, rather, suggests to those who use it a bright vision of a world where things will be far better than they are now.[9]

F. E. Manuel and F. P. Manuel observe:

> The descriptive and the discursive rhetorical modes in utopia are never, or rarely ever, found in a simon-pure state, since the living portrait of a utopia rests on a set of implicit psychological, philosophical, or theological assumptions about the nature of man [*sic*], and the discursive exposition of utopian principles frequently has recourse to illustrations from ordinary events, proposed hypothetical situations, and analogies from other realms of being. In the course of time, "proper" utopias, discussions of utopian thought, and portrayals of utopian states of consciousness have so interpenetrated that the perimeters of the concept of utopia have to be left hazy.[10]

Following Manuel and Manuel, this study presupposes a "utopian propensity" in humankind,[11] which comprehends diverse, although often overlapping and interrelated, traditions, philosophies, cultures, images, aims, desires, and literary genres. For heuristic purposes, the classification schemes for Graeco-Roman utopias suggested by Doyne Dawson[12] and for biblical utopias by John J. Collins[13] are adapted in subsequent chapters.

The consideration of Jesus' *basileia* teaching and the movement within which it functioned are preceded by four chapters. Chapter 1, on ancient, classical, and hellenistic utopias, examines mythical, para-disal, and fantastic utopias, including the myth of the golden age of Kronos; the Elysian Fields and the Islands of the Blessed; the myth of Atlantis; hellenistic utopian romances; philosophical proposals for ideal city-states (notably, Plato's *Republic* and Aristotle's *Politics*); Aristophanes' comic gynocratic utopia, the *Ecclesiazusai;* the ideal-ized societies of Sparta and Athens; and the few surviving accounts of ancient attempts to form societies built on utopian principles.

Chapter 2, on biblical and early Jewish utopias, covers the myth of Eden and its biblical and early Jewish developments, and idealized portrayals of the land of Israel, both temporal/locative (idealizations of the land and of eras in Israel's history) and legal/covenantal utopias (idealizations of Torah). The temporal/locative utopias include bibli-cal formulations of an agrarian Israel as the "land of milk and honey" and the land promised to the ancestors; the idealized era of the united monarchy under David and Solomon, when "Judah and Israel dwelt safely, every man under his vine and under his fig tree, from Dan to Beer-Sheba, all the days of Solomon" (1 Kgs 5:5), and its messianic developments; prophetic and apocalyptic idealizations of Jerusalem and the Temple; literary "maps" of the ideal boundaries of the land of Israel; depictions of Torah as the optimum national constitution and of Moses as the consummate lawgiver; the laws of Jubilee; and dynamic-theocratic traditions of divine kingship, from ancient Near Eastern myth to biblical and postbiblical expressions, especially in the Psalms and apocalyptic literature.

Chapter 3 examines the (possibly unique) phenomenon of the formation of utopian communities in early Judaism, especially the Essenes, a Palestinian movement described by Pliny the Elder, Philo, and Josephus, and widely associated with the Dead Sea Scrolls, and the Therapeutai, a group of Egyptian Jewish monastic philosophers known to us only from Philo's *On the Contemplative Life.* This the Baptist, Jesus and his circle, and the early *basileia* movement that endured after their martyrdoms. Of course, this does not obviate the need for critical evaluation of the evidence, which, as Paula Fredriksen notes, is gleaned from early Christian writings: *"all* . . . written from a post-Resurrection perspective, which in turn refracts what historical reminiscences they contain."[23]

Most important, the resulting portrait of Jesus and the *basileia* movement is a reconstruction informed by Graeco-Roman, biblical, and Jewish utopian traditions, a body of material that has not previously been juxtaposed with Jesus' kingdom teaching. That is, the model of Jesus and the kingdom that emerges in chapter 5 grows out of the hypothesis that *hē basileia tou theou* is one of many ancient utopian/eutopian visions, and that Jesus and his circle shared some of the "utopian propensities" of their contemporaries, both Jewish and non-Jewish. As such, it is, as John P. Meier put it, a "scientific construct, a theoretical abstraction of modern scholars that coincides partially with the real Jesus of Nazareth."[24] Like any other academic model of the historical Jesus, it is also the product of the scholarly imagination, intuition, and predispositions of the author, and it should be read with these factors in mind. I hope that, despite these limitations (or perhaps because of them), this study offers a distinctive, plausible, and illuminating perspective on Jesus and the kingdom of God.

ANCIENT, CLASSICAL, *and* HELLENISTIC UTOPIAS

ncient literature, especially Greek, is rich with utopian traditions of different kinds that were widespread in their time. In Aristophanes' comic play *Ecclesiazusai* (455 BCE), one of the characters quips that entrusting the governance of the state to women is the only innovation that Athens has not yet tried. In the *Politics*, Aristotle (fourth century BCE) remarks that many private persons, philosophers, and statesmen had proposed constitutional innovations before Plato (although none of their ideas had been as outlandish as Plato's) (2,7).

For the purpose of sorting through the various genres of Greek utopian literature, Doyne Dawson's typology is helpful:

1. Mythological, fantastic and messianic works, e.g., legends of the golden age and the Elysian Fields (Homer, Hesiod), literary adaptations of such myths, and fantastic history and geography.

2. Political utopian works, subclassified into two genres:

    a. "Low" utopianism. Works of political philosophy such as Plato's *Laws*, Aristotle's *Politics* 7–8, and *On the Republic* and *On the Laws* by Cicero, which develop comprehensive programs for the ideal city-state meant to be put into practice if possible.

    b. "High" utopianism. These are works of political philosophy that propose an ideal city-state not meant to be literally implemented, meant as models for political reform; Plato's *Republic* is the prime example.[1]

In this chapter, Dawson's schema will be used as a rough outline for an examination of ancient utopias that may have affinities with biblical traditions. The works discussed below have been selected as representative of larger bodies of utopian thinking and for their comparability to elements in Israelite-Jewish literature. While some obvious biblical and Jewish parallels will be adduced in this chapter, chapters 2 and 3 will be devoted primarily to biblical and early Jewish utopian traditions.

Mythical, Paradisal, and Fantastic Utopias

THE GOLDEN AGE OF KRONOS

The oldest extant account of a mythical utopia in the Greek tradition (c. 750 BCE) is found in Hesiod's *Works and Days* (106–200).[2] According to Hesiod, the gods and humanity sprang from the same (unidentified) source. The Olympian gods created the human race, who lived in a golden age ruled by the Titan Kronos. This first generation of human beings lived a joyful, ageless life, feasting and enjoying the bounty of the earth, "rich in flocks and loved by the blessed gods." When they died, it was as if they had merely fallen asleep, and their spirits lived on as kindly guardians of humanity.

    In ancient Rome, the Saturnalia was a joyous winter solstice festival that Catullus called the "best of days" (14.15); it commemorated the age of Kronos (Saturn), with a formal sacrifice at the temple of the god, banqueting, relaxation, casual dress, and gift giving. Masters waited on slaves, symbolizing the displacement of the Cthonic gods by the Olympians. Slaves enjoyed a temporary holiday from their duties, and they were allowed to gamble. The regard in which the festival was held is illustrated by the Roman poet Statius (first century CE), who wrote, "Time shall not destroy that Holy Day, so long as the hills of Latium endure and Father Tiber, while your city of Roma and the Capitol remain."[3]

According to Hesiod, subsequent generations of mortals were far less noble than those of the race of Kronos. The people of the silver age (*Works and Days* 130–40) enjoyed a childhood of a hundred years, but their adult lives were brief, and they were inclined to sinfulness and impiety. Nonetheless, they are honored as "divine spirits of the underworld" by mortals. Kronos's son Zeus was the divine father of the third, brazen race (*Works and Days* 145–55), named after their brass houses, armor, weapons, and implements. They were even less worthy than the silver generation, very strong and warlike, ultimately destroyed by their own violence. Their eternal fate was to descend into Hades and to leave no name.

Among the ancient tradents of the ages/races of humanity, only Hesiod includes a fourth, heroic generation (*Works and Days* 160–70), nobler and more righteous than the brazen race, populated by demigods; some of these heroes did not die but were granted eternal life by Zeus in the Islands of the Blessed, where they live on in bliss and are honored and glorified by mortals. The fifth age of humanity, the race of iron (*Works and Days* 174–200), is the one of Hesiod's time, the most unfortunate generation, marked by constant labor and sorrow, strife among friends and family members, irreverence, injustice, and sin. The people of the iron age are so wretched that Aidōs (Shame, Decency) and Nemesis (Retribution, Divine Justice) will forsake humanity altogether, leaving them nothing but sorrow and injustice.

In the Hebrew Bible, the more usual sequence of four ages (golden, silver, bronze, and iron) is reflected in the dream of Nebuchadnezzar recorded in the book of Daniel (Dan 2:31-35). In the dream the king sees a giant, dazzling statue with a head of gold, chest and arms of silver, midriff and thighs of bronze, and feet of iron and clay. A stone, not cut by human hands, is cast at the figure, which breaks apart and disintegrates; the stone grows into a great mountain that fills the whole earth. Daniel explains to the king that the golden head of the statue represents his own God-given realm (2:36–38); the silver, bronze, and iron/clay parts are future, inferior kingdoms, the last of which will be divided and unstable (2:39–43). These probably represent Media (silver), Persia (bronze), and Greece (iron and clay), whose imperial power was divided after the death of Alexander the Great (323 BCE). The stone/mountain is the kingdom of the God of heaven, which will never be destroyed, "nor shall this kingdom be left to another people" (Dan 2:44). The Danielic prophecy is widely acknowledged to be a Jewish apocalyptic adaptation (and allegorization) of the myth of the four (or five) ages of the world.

In the first century BCE, the Roman poet Virgil celebrated the dawn of a new golden age to be initiated by the birth of an infant prodigy:

> Now is come the last age of Cumaean song; the great line of the centuries begins anew. Now the Virgin returns, the reign of Saturn returns; now a new generation descends from heaven on high. Only do you, pure Lucina, smile on the birth of the child, under whom the iron brood shall at last cease and a golden race spring up throughout the world! Your own Apollo now is king!
>
> And in your consulship, Pollio, yes, yours, shall this glorious age begin, and the mighty months commence on their march. . . . He shall have the gift of divine life, shall see heroes mingled with gods, and shall himself be seen by them, and shall rule the world to which his father's prowess brought peace.
>
> But for you, child, the earth untilled will pour forth its first pretty gifts, gadding ivy with foxglove everywhere, and the Egyptian bean blended with the laughing briar; unbidden it will pour fourth for you a cradle of smiling flowers.

Unbidden, the goats will bring home their udders swollen
with milk, and the cattle will not fear huge lions. The ser-
pent, too, will perish, and perish will the plant that hides its
poison; Assyrian spice will spring up on every soil. . . .

Next, when now the strength of years has made you a
man, even the trader will quit the sea, nor will the ship of
pine exchange wares; every land will bear all fruits. Earth
will not suffer the harrow, nor the vine the pruning hoe;
the sturdy ploughman, too, will now loose his oxen from
the yoke. No more will wool be taught to put on varied
hues, but of himself the ram in the meadows will change
his fleece, now to sweetly blushing purple, now to a saffron
yellow; and scarlet shall clothe the grazing lambs at will.

"Ages so blessed, glide on!" cried the Fates to their spin-
dles, voicing in unison the Fixed will of Destiny.[4]

This historicizing Roman propaganda, dated to circa 40 BCE around
the time of the pact between Octavian (Augustus) and Mark Antony,
presaged the Augustan peace, which, as John Dominic Crossan
observes, devolves in the works of Roman poets and historians from
"peace as the whole earth ecstatic with fertility, to peace as the victory
of West over East, to peace as the still center of a permanently war-torn
periphery" (cf. Propertius, *Elegies* 2.16, 4.6; Virgil, *Aeneid* 8.678–700;
Horace, *Odes* 1.21, 35; Tacitus, *Agricola* 30–31).[5]

THE ELYSIAN FIELDS AND THE ISLANDS OF THE BLESSED

While the golden age of Kronos is enjoyed by a race of long-lived mortals on the surface of the earth, the Elysian fields, first mentioned in
Homer (*Odyssey* 4, 561–69), are a deathless haven for certain heroes
(like Menelaus, son-in-law of Zeus). Neither Hades nor Olympus,
the Elysian fields are "at the world's end . . . the land where living is
made easy for mankind, where no snow falls, no strong winds blow
and there is never any rain, but day after day the West Wind's tuneful
breeze comes in from the Ocean to refresh its people."[6] In Hesiod's
telling of the myth, Kronos became the ruler of the Islands of the
Blessed when he was deposed by his son Zeus. There, the departed

heroes dwell, under conditions similar to those enjoyed during the golden age, with hearts "free of sorrow," fed by the delicious fruits of the earth that grow anew three times a year (*Works and Days* 169–73). For the Orphic poet Pindar (fifth century BCE),[7] the Islands of the Blessed become the final, post-Elysian reward of a select group of initiates purified of sin through the transmigration of souls.[8] As Manuel and Manuel observe, Pindar's account of the final abode of pure souls is more elaborate than those of his predecessors:

> The cooling ocean breezes of this abode of the pure recall Homer and Hesiod, but the environment has been newly enriched. Radiant trees and flowers of gold blaze all about and the blessed ones entwine their arms and crown their heads with chaplets. According to a threnody that has been related to the ode, the immortal souls are more sportive than in the passive Homeric Elysium: "Some there delight themselves with feats of horsemanship and the athlete's practicings. Some with draught-play, others with the music of lyres."[9]

While Plato (fourth century BCE) accepted the Orphic doctrine of triple incarnations and final release of the soul for the true philosopher, he ridiculed the material rewards of the afterlife celebrated by some Orphic poets, like Musaeus and Eumolpus, who envision Elysium as a banquet where the blessed recline on couches, crowned with wreaths, enjoying endless cups of wine.[10] Later writers, like Plutarch (first century CE), locate the blessed realm where Persephone presides over the souls of the righteous on the moon (*Moralia 12: Concerning the Face Which Appears on the Face of the Moon*).[11]

THE MYTH OF ATLANTIS AND THE HELLENISTIC UTOPIAS

The famous lost island continent of Atlantis is mentioned briefly in Plato's *Timaeus* (25a–d) and at greater length in his *Critias* (113c–121c). In both works, it is juxtaposed with the Athens of remote antiquity. Atlantis was the realm of Poseidon's human descendants, lavishly stocked with animal and plant life, including foodstuffs that grew spontaneously in wonderful abundance. A precious metal called ori-alchum, second only to gold in value, was found there and nowhere else. The Atlantean metropolis was carefully and intricately planned, and densely populated; the countryside was mountainous, filled with wealthy rural folk, and blessed with rivers, lakes, and meadows that amply supported both humans and animals—even elephants. The people were governed by ten kings descended from the god, absolute monarchs with the power of life and death over their subjects. The kings also had a sacerdotal function: they periodically offered a bull sacrifice to Poseidon, which reinforced their allegiance to the laws, inscribed on the pillar of the god's temple, bequeathed by their divine ancestor. Only by consensus of the ten kings could a sentence of death be imposed on any citizen of the country.

Atlantis was a great and powerful empire, which attempted to con-quer archaic Athens. However, both ancient powers were destroyed by earthquakes and floods; the warlike Athenians were swallowed up by the earth, while the island continent disappeared into the sea (*Timaeus* 25d). Plato attributes the destruction of Atlantis to the decline in godlike virtue among its inhabitants. As long as the divine nature remained strong in them, they cared little for material wealth, despis-ing everything but virtue. When the human element in the Atlanteans began to gain the upper hand over the divine, they became disgruntled with their lot and behaved in shameful ways, although to the super-ficial observer they still seemed blessed and glorious (*Critias* 121b). The fragmentary *Critias* ends abruptly with a divine council called by the high god Zeus, who has seen the moral decline in the Atlanteans and plans to chastise them, presumably with the deluge described in *Timaeus*.[12]

Compared to Plato's moral fable, the hellenistic tales of ideal soci-eties set in distant locales like Panchaïa, Hyperborea, and the Islands of the Sun seem to have been written more to amaze and entertain than to convey philosophical truth.[13] The utopian romances only sur-vive in fragments or in the testimonies of later authors, and they are cast as travel narratives claiming to relate the observations of visi-tors to remote parts of the world.[14] A novel attributed to Euhemerus of Messene (c. 300 BCE),[15] the *Sacred History* (*Hiera Anagraphē*),[16] recounts the journey of the author to an unknown island in the Indian Ocean, where he found, inscribed on a stele in the temple of Zeus, an explanation of the origin of religion. The utopian isle, Panchaïa ("All Good"), a land rich in agricultural and mineral resources, had been settled by the Cretan king Zeus, later deified by his people. The society was made up of three castes: priests/artisans, farmers, and soldiers/shepherds. Slaves are not mentioned. The castes were given roughly equal status, although the priests had the last word in the running of the community, enjoyed a higher standard of living than the others, and lived in a sacred precinct called Panara. Homes and gardens were privately owned, but all production and revenues were allotted by the priests to the citizens, with the priests retaining a double share. Trade with the outside world was limited, and the export of minerals was forbidden. Panchaïan society was perfectly functional, perhaps reflecting the urban planning ideas of Hippodamus of Miletus,[17] and multi-ethnic, made up of "indigenous Panchaïans . . . immigrant Scythians, Cretans, Indians, and Oceanites,"[18] all of whom enjoyed citizenship. The method of governance was a mixture of monarchy and democracy. Manuel and Manuel describe Panchaïa as "the syncretism of Greek and Asiatic elements that Alexander himself had dreamed of—an Oriental environment and Greek principles."[19]

Several ancient authors preserve traditions about the land of the Hyperboreans (Theopompus, Hecataeus of Abdera,[20] Diodorus Siculus, Aelian, Pliny the Elder, Pomponius Mela); the following account borrows elements from the various writers.[21] The Hyperboreans live beyond the North Wind on a large island and worship Apollo, for whom they built a magnificent temple. The climate is mild and harvests regular, so the inhabitants have time for playing music and singing hymns. Greeks of ancient times journeyed there and left extravagant gifts. The god himself visits the island every nineteen years, corresponding with the cycles of the stars: "At the time of this appearance of the god he both plays on the cithara and dances continuously the night through from the vernal equinox until the rising of the Pleiades, expressing in this matter his delight in his successes" (Diodorus Siculus 2.47).[22] Aelian adds a vivid description of the magnificence of Hyperborean worship: the priests of Apollo are three descendants of Boreas and Chione; during the ritual of the god, clouds of swans swoop down, purifying the temple by circling it, after which they descend into the temple precinct. The swans join in harmoniously with the songs of the worshipers, who sing and praise the god all day long, after which the birds depart.[23] Pomponius Mela (first century CE) asserts that the Hyperboreans live without agriculture off the spontaneous produce of the earth; they enjoy long lives and die when they reach "sufficiency of living" (*satietas*), at which point they joyously hurl themselves into the sea.[24] Pliny the Elder (first century CE) holds that "they sow in the morning periods, reap at midday, pluck the fruit from the trees at sunset, and retire into caves for the night" in their cycle of six-month days.[25]

The southern counterparts of the Hyperboreans are the Ethiopians, whose realm serves as a retreat for the Olympian gods, to give them respite from "attending the needs and sufferings of strife-worn humans."[26] In a scene between a Persian emissary and the Ethiopian king, Herodotus highlights the difference between the "civilized" world and the natural life of the Ethiopians: the clothing they wear is simple and organic, rather than dyed; they use metals for practical purposes, rather than for useless golden jewelry; they scorn fragrant ointments like myrrh; they eat simple dishes rather than feeding on bread baked from grain grown in dung-enriched soil (*Histories* 3.23).[27] James S. Romm argues that Herodotus used the Ethiopians as a foil for the artificial life of the Greeks:

> The most esteemed products of a sophisticated, manufacturing-based society suddenly lose their value when viewed through the eyes of *Naturvölker*, for whom the raw materials supplied by nature are sufficient to meet every need.... [The Ethiopian king] exhibits their food and drink (boiled meat and milk); the spring of rarefied water which gives a glossy sheen, "like that of olive oil," to those who bathe in it; the prison, where wrongdoers are bound in golden fetters; and lastly the famous meat-producing Table of the Sun. In each case the Ethiopians are seen to obtain from the environment around them the substances which the Persians can only get, ignobly, by manufacture or cultivation.[28]

When introduced to palm wine, it is accepted as a health-giving drink, since "in their golden-age innocence, they do not crave it immoderately."[29] When the Ethiopians die, they are entombed in crystalline chambers made of a stone called *huelos*, which miraculously preserves the bodies of the deceased so that their families and friends can view them and make the appropriate sacrifices.[30] Romm concludes that "like their Homeric antecedents, . . . Herodotus' Ethiopians inhabit a landscape which, with its supernatural abundance, brings them close in stature to the gods."[31]

The tale of Iamubulus's journey to the islands of the sun is preserved fragmentarily in Diodorus Siculus (2.55–59). Iambulus is a young merchant who is seized by brigands and abandoned in Ethiopia. As part of a ritual to purify their land, the Ethiopians send the captive and a companion off in a boat, ordering them to sail until they find a blessed isle inhabited by virtuous people. After four months, they reach such an island, where the natives welcome them. The isle is one of seven, all of them perfectly spherical and similar in size, located at the equator. The inhabitants of the islands all practice the same customs. The climate is temperate, and food is abundant. Day and night are of equal length, and the constellations are entirely different. Clothing is made easily from local reeds and dyed purple with pounded oyster shells, so that everyone is clad royally. The people are over six feet tall, very strong, with flexible bones, and hairless except for that which covers their heads and faces. Their ears are large, with valve-like coverings, and their tongues are divided so that they can speak every language, imitate any bird, and carry on two conversations at once. They live in clans of not more than four hundred members and ruled by the oldest man, who is obeyed by everyone. The leader commits suicide when he reaches the age of 150, and the next oldest succeeds him. The people serve one another, performing necessary duties in rotation. Marriage is unknown, and children are raised as much-loved wards of the community. Communal harmony is their highest goal. Babies are tested as to whether they are worthy of life by being made to ride on the backs of giant birds; those who fail the test are cast out of the community as unlikely to survive long. Despite the abundance of their environment, the Heliopolitans live simple lives and eat only what they need. While they eat meat and cooked foods, they do not indulge in sauces and condiments. Certain days are specified for the consumption of certain foods. The people are long-lived and free of disease. Those who are maimed must commit suicide, as must everyone else when they reach the age of 150. This is accomplished voluntarily and painlessly with the aid of a soporific plant. The dead are buried simply and naturally. These people worship the heavens, the celestial bodies, and especially the sun, which they celebrate with hymns and songs. They have a strange alphabet and pursue all learning enthusiastically, especially astronomy. They have a peculiar, small animal whose blood has miraculous healing properties; its blood can be used to glue a severed, nonvital body part back on if the cut is fresh. After seven years with the islanders, Iambulus and his companion are forced to leave on account of their evil ways.[32]

These fantastic romances seem far removed from the concerns of formative Judaism and Christianity. However, it will be argued in subsequent chapters that two early Jewish sectarian groups, the Essenes and the Therapeutai, show affinities with the kinds of utopian visions developed in such works.

Plato's Republic and Aristotle's Politics

According to Dawson's typology, Plato's *Republic* is the best-known and oldest example of a "high" utopia, a political-philosophical proposal for an ideal city-state not designed actually to be implemented, but meant as a model for political reform.[33] In contrast, Artistotle's *Politics* 7–8 sketches a paradigmatic "low utopia," a comprehensive program for an ideal *polis* to be put into practice if possible.[34] For purposes of comparison, the utopian schemes of the two philosophers will be presented together.

The outlines of Plato's ideal city-state as developed in the *Republic* 2.369–8.544 are well known. Citizens are divided into two main classes: laborers and guardians,[35] the latter of which is subdivided into rulers and auxiliaries (soldiers). Class is determined not by birth but by aptitude and ability. The educational system is carefully designed to produce able and healthy members dedicated to the welfare and defense of the state and of each other.[36] Indoctrination and censorship are used to control thought and behaviors. All property, including women and children, is held in common (*koinonia*); an androcentric way of saying that the patriarchal household would be abolished. Members of the guardian class dine communally (*syssitia*). Couplings between eugenically selected women and men of suitable ages are temporary and carefully regulated; children are reared away from their parents by specialists. Infants with undesirable qualities are euthanized. As a safeguard against incest, men and women regard children of a certain age-range as "kin" (a custom that seems to allow for brother-sister mating).[37] The guardians, particularly, regard any peer they meet as "a brother or sister, father or mother, son or daughter, grandparent or grandchild" (465). Women and men are reared and trained for the same occupations, with some provision for women's lesser physical (and possibly intellectual) strength.[38]

For Dawson, the utopian *polis* sketched above remains a "low utopia," that is, one that is designed to be implemented.[39] Plato's "high" or purely idealistic utopia is found in *Republic* 5.473–8.544, which deals with the rule of philosophers that would result in the "heavenly city, the rule of the wise."[40] Potential philosopher-rulers of both sexes would receive an extensive and rigorous program of philosophical and practical education until they reached the age of fifty; at this point, if they were capable of perceiving the good, they would be qualified to take turns with their colleagues in attending to the governance of the state (7.540a). As Ferguson puts it, "Political troubles will persist until philosophers become rulers or rulers take seriously to the study of philosophy, that is until political authority and the pursuit of wisdom coincide" (*Rep.* 5,473 C–D).[41] Their reward after death would be posthumous honors from the state, promotion to either divine or godlike status, and translation to the Islands of the Blessed (7.540c). The dialogue ends with the implication that the social order sketched by Socrates is more than an idle dream, although it would be extremely difficult to attain (7.541d), followed by a summary of the constitution of the ideal state (8.543–44), which serves as a transition to the description of imperfect societies (8.545–9.592).

In general, Aristotle is not a utopian thinker but rather a philosopher concerned with analyzing existing constitutions in order to give sound political advice to existing states.[42] *Politics* 2.1–6 is devoted to a critique of Plato's ideal state as outlined in the *Republic*, especially with regard to community of wives and children (2.1–4) and of property (2.5). For Aristotle, the fundamental unit of the state is the patriarchal household (1.2–3):

> Seeing then that the state is made up of households, before speaking of the state we must speak of the management of the household. The parts of household management correspond to the persons who compose the household, and a complete household consists of slaves and freemen. Now we should begin by examining everything in its fewest possible elements; and the first and fewest possible parts of a family are master and slave, husband and wife, father and children. We have therefore to consider what each of these three relations is and ought to be: I mean the relation of master and servant, the marriage relation (the conjunction of man and wife has no name of its own), and thirdly, the procreative relation (this also has no proper name). And there is another element of a household, the so-called art of getting wealth, which, according to some, is identical with household management, according to others, a principal part of it; the nature of this art will also have to be considered by us. (1.3)[43]

The relationships of the hierarchically organized family—including the rule of masters over slaves and of husbands over wives—is natural and permanent (1.5–7, 12):

> For that some should rule and others be ruled is a thing not only necessary, but expedient; from the hour of their birth, some are marked out for subjection, others for rule. . . . Although there may be exceptions to the order of nature, the male is by nature fitter for command than the female,

> just as the elder and full-grown is superior to the younger
> and more immature. . . . The relation of the male to the
> female is of this kind, but there the inequality is perma-
> nent. (1.5, 12)

Therefore, communistic schemes like that espoused by the fictive
Socrates in the *Republic* and later Cynic and Stoic philosophies, which
dispense with the household in different ways,[44] are contrary to nature
and unsustainable.

Aristotle's own proposal for the optimum state, classified as a "low
utopia" by Dawson,[45] is found in *Politics* 7–8. Citizenship is restricted
to landowners, who are required to devote themselves solely to the
higher callings of war, religion, and government. There is a com-
pulsory public education system,[46] and the male citizens, like the
Spartans, eat at a common mess (*syssitia*). Public slaves of barbarian
origin should supply all other labor, since the nonhellenic races are
inclined to servility by their nature (7.7). The patriarchal household
remains fundamental, but marriage and the family are strictly regulated: couples must marry at the optimum ages (for men, thirty-
seven, for women, eighteen); pregnant women must be solicitous
of their health; population size is limited by abortion when couples
have "children in excess" (7.16);[47] adultery for both husband and wife
is deplored.

As Dawson observes, this Aristotelian utopia (like Plato's) has
many affinities with the Spartan model of "a separate soldier class
and common meals. . . . Like Plato, he thought the ideal city would be a
broad-based oligarchy, as collectivistic as the Spartan and more sexu-
ally puritanical."[48] Aristotle's greatest divergences from Plato are in his
insistence on retaining the patriarchal *oikos* and private property[49]
and in his conviction that men and women are different by nature,[50]
which necessitates distinct gender roles and supports the traditional
family. Not surprisingly, the Cynics, who rejected the household altogether in order to pursue the simple, peripatetic life, and the Stoics,
whose utopian ideal rejected the family and kinship in favor of the
fellowship of the wise,[51] were both open to the admission of women
philosophers.[52]

Aristophanes' Ecclesiazusai:
A Comic Utopia

Prior to Plato's *Republic*, there is one prominent example of an imagined city-state that dispenses with private property and the household, and that grants equality—even dominance—to women. This is the comic play *Ecclesiazusai* ("Women of the Assembly") of Aristophanes (c. 393 BCE). Dawson neatly summarizes the main points of the utopian gynocracy:

> The women of Athens decide to take over the polis. They disguise themselves as men, pack the assembly, and push through a resolution to turn over all affairs of government to the women, on the grounds that everything else has been tried (456). Once in power, their leader Praxagora ("Busy in the Marketplace") realizes that to stay there she must propose some unheard-of novelty (578ff.). Therefore it is decreed that all things are to be held in common (*koinonein*), and all the citizens to have a common (*koinon*) and equal (*homoios*) way of life; all property, both land and movables, will be put into a common store; all individual *oikoi* (households) will be knocked together into a communal dwelling; all citizens will eat at *syssitia*; gold and silver will be forbidden; all slaves will be publicly owned and will do the work presently done by poor citizens, leaving the entire [remaining] citizen body to live in leisure; lawsuits will disappear and the courts of law will be turned into banquet halls. It is taken for granted that this system of communal property will entail the abolition of the family and the communal raising of children, who will regard all older people as their parents. The resulting sexual promiscuity will be curbed only by the principle of equality in pleasure, which is ensured by regulations favoring the old and ugly in sexual competition; this last is called a particularly "democratic" proposal (631, 945).[53]

The ideal republics of Praxagora and Plato contain the following common elements: community of property (*koinonia tōn ktēmatōn*); community of women (*koinonia tōn gynaikōn*) or "communism in sex, marriage, and family"; and sexual equality, with women and men consistently enjoying the same prerogatives.[54]

Opinions differ as to the possible relationship between Aristophanes' comic fantasy and Plato's ideal state. Ferguson mentions in passing that the equality of the sexes was "a proposition almost unthinkable except for purposes of comic fantasy at Athens, and not remotely practiced politically anywhere else in the Greek world,"[55] perhaps implying that Plato was familiar with the *Ecclesiazusai* and adapted its outrageous premise for his own more serious purposes. Dawson surmises that Aristophanes' audience was already familiar with the ideas of "community of goods and women" from traditions about the societies of remote barbarians and Sophistic admiration for these practices: "It may have been already a rhetorical commonplace, useful to any moralist who wanted to shame the Athenians by pointing to the superior *koinonia* practiced by various foreigners."[56] These legends of barbarian communism may have been blended with the ancient admiration for the Spartans, who "were well known to have certain communistic attitudes toward property and women."[57] Other possibilities are that there was a pre-Aristophanic philosophical tradition that posited proto-feminist political reform[58] or that Plato was influenced by female philosophers in his own circle.[59]

Idealized Societies, Utopian Experiments

As implied above, Sparta was widely admired in antiquity for its unique constitution.[60] The legendary lawgiver Lycurgus was reputed to have devised the uniquely Spartan (Laconian, Lacedaemonian) military class-stratified social order that included state control over private property, limited equality between the sexes, the regulation of sex and marriage (for eugenic purposes), public education (for both sexes), common meals (for men), uniform attire, laws against luxurious buildings, limited and simple legislation, what Aristotle called "a happy mixture of democracy and oligarchy" (*Politics* 1294b), deliberately limited territory, and resistance to change as a sign of imperfection.[61] Many ancient political philosophers, including (by Plato's account) Socrates, Plato, and Aristotle, admired the Spartan system and integrated aspects of it into their ideal societies.[62] The utopias envisioned in the Hellenistic romances also show some Spartan affinities, perhaps as mediated by their philosophical admirers.[63] Josephus contrasts the laws propagated by Lycurgus, so widely admired for their antiquity, with the laws of Moses, which, he asserted, had endured for more than two thousand years under the most turbulent and trying circumstances (*Against Apion* 2.23–25; cf. 2.16).[64]

The other ancient lawgiver whose regime is described in utopian terms by some ancient writers is Solon (sixth century BCE), the reputed founder of Athenian democracy. The contributions of the historical Solon, fragments of whose poetry are extant,[65] were probably moderate and practical:

> Solon cancelled outstanding debts and mortgages . . . and abolished borrowing on the security of the person, and thus with one stroke ended serfdom in Attica. He produced a series of economic measures directed to the encouragement of trade and industry. He modified the archaic severity of the legal code. He produced constitutional reforms based on property qualifications, which left the power in the hands of the rich, but diffused beyond the old aristocracy and limited, and gave the commoners rights which were to prove the source and origin of the later democracy. He was not himself an extreme democrat—indeed he was not himself an extreme of any sort.[66]

The excellence of Athenian democracy is idealized in the Periclean funeral oration of Thucydides (died c. 460 BCE) and Plutarch's *Life of Solon* (first century CE).[67] The Greek historian places an encomium to Athenian democracy on the lips of the fallen hero Pericles:

> Our constitution does not copy the laws of neighbouring states; we are rather a pattern to others than imitators

ourselves. Its administration favours the many instead of the few; this is why it is called a democracy. If we look to the laws, they afford equal justice to all in their private differences; if no social standing, advancement in public life falls to reputation for capacity, class considerations not being allowed to interfere with merit; nor again does poverty bar the way, if a man is able to serve the state, he is not hindered by the obscurity of his condition. The freedom which we enjoy in our government extends also to our ordinary life. There, far from exercising a jealous surveillance over each other, we do not feel called upon to be angry with our neighbour for doing what he likes, or even to indulge in those injurious looks which cannot fail to be offensive, although they inflict no positive penalty. But all this ease in our private relations does not make us lawless as citizens. Against this fear is our chief safeguard, teaching us to obey the magistrates and the laws, particularly such as regard the protection of the injured, whether they are actually on the statute book, or belong to that code which, although unwritten, yet cannot be broken without acknowledged disgrace. (Thucydides, *History*, 2,6)[68]

Plutarch places an aretalogy on the lawgiver's lips:

> For to the common people I gave so much power as is sufficient,
> Neither robbing them of dignity, nor giving them too much;
> And those who had power, and were marvellously rich,
> Even for these I contrived that they suffered no harm.
> I stood with a mighty shield in front of both classes,
> And suffered neither of them to prevail unjustly.[69]

As Manuel and Manuel note, in the West the democratic and authoritarian constitutional ideals represented by Athens and Sparta have become representatives of "contradictory ways of life, different psychologies, opposing views of the optimum society."[70] In antiquity, the extant evidence indicates than the "ascetic and communistic" Spartan model was often preferred to the "loosely democratic" state, which was "tolerant of sensate pleasure" and associated with Solon.[71]

In the Greek tradition, very few examples of deliberate attempts to establish communities founded on utopian principles are mentioned. The Pythagoreans (sixth century BCE) are reputed to have lived in communistic associations supported by a political theory that held up this way of life as a model for society as a whole, possibly influencing Plato's *Republic*.[72] However, most of the evidence of Pythagorean political utopianism comes from neo-Pythagoreans of the Roman Empire, especially Iamblichus's *Life of Pythagoras* (c. 300 CE).[73] Dawson concludes that while the Pythagoreans probably organized in cult organizations (*thiasoi*), there was "never any sort of utopia; and if there was ever a Pythagorean political theory, there is no reason to suppose it had any connection with the Pythagorean common life."[74] More like a religious order than a utopian community, the *thiasos* probably grew out of Pythagorean dietary regulations, which were conducive to common meals; members would be expected to contribute some of their property to provide the food.[75] The Pythagoreans maintained separate households and did not make sex, marriage, and family communal, although women were admitted to their associations, and adultery was forbidden to men as well as women.[76]

Scanty accounts of one possible ancient utopian experiment, the *Ouranopolis* ("City of Heaven") of Alexarchus, the brother of Cassander of Macedonia (c. 355–297 BCE), are preserved by Athenaeus (3.98D) (c. 200 BCE; cf. Strabo, *Geography* 7.1.162). Alexarchus is supposed to have imposed an odd and archaic form of the Greek language on the new *polis*; it was said that he "transformed himself into the sun, that he wrote a letter in which Dionysus was identified with the Egyptian Arsaphes, and that Uranopolis was on the isthmus linking Athos with the mainland, near where Xerxes tried to dig his canal; it had a circuit of thirty states, or about four miles."[77] Coins belonging to the city are extant, naming the citizens of the polis

Ouranidai ("Children of Heaven"), bearing the figure of the divine patron Aphrodite Ourania, whose worship there probably predated the founding of the city.[78] Ferguson regards the founding of Ouranopolis by an associate of Euhemerus of Messene (whose mythical Panchaïa is sketched above) as suggestive:

> We have a city of an unusual name, the City of Heaven, citizens uniquely called Children of Heaven, a ruler identified with the sun, a patron-goddess who provides a link with the Near East and who is in some circles associated with ethical ideas, a deal of astral symbolism, and a new language. This emerges from the same circle as a rationalist who produces a theoretical Utopia with similar astral symbolism, a similar attempt to depict a community which reaches out beyond the traditional Greek boundaries, a clear power structure, and interesting economic provisions.[79]

Unfortunately, too little is known of the constitution of Ouranopolis to determine whether it was modeled on Euhemerus's Panchaïa, or if it was, in fact, as Ferguson suggests "a practical attempt to produce a foundation of a new kind to incorporate the values of a new age."[80] We shall see in subsequent chapters that the best-attested examples of ancient communities actually founded on utopian principles are Jewish.

BIBLICAL UTOPIAS:
FROM EDEN *to the* KINGDOM *of* GOD

s noted in the introduction, little scholarship has been devoted to the utopian themes that run through the Hebrew Bible,[1] and which are transformed in the literature of Second Temple Judaism and the early Christian scriptures. Binyamin Uffenheimer finds two main types of biblical utopia: "the ancient one, which is weaved into the existing social fabric; the second type is very common in prophetic literature . . . essentially presenting those expectations which have failed in history."[2] John J. Collins cites Jonathan Z. Smith's opinion that the biblical vision of the world is "locative" rather than "utopian," that is, the biblical authors emphasize *place*, the land of Israel, rather than "no place" (the literal sense of utopia, *ou-topos*).[3] Rather than relying on the Greek etymology of the term *utopia*, Collins cites the modern usage as shaped by Sir Thomas More, which refers to "an ideal society . . . where all things are well [*eu-topia*]."[4] Using this definition as a guide, Collins finds four main strands of biblical utopian thinking:

The first, which envisions a transformed land of Israel, may be termed agricultural. The second, which focuses on an ideal Jerusalem, has an urban character. The third is the model of an ideal community, such as we find in the Dead Sea Scrolls and in the writings of Philo. The fourth, which appears at the beginning of Genesis and again in apocalyptic visions at the end of the biblical period, is properly utopian in the sense that the place it imagines is out of this world.[5]

In contrast to Greek utopias, the Israelite-Jewish tradition usually imagines the optimum society as located in the land of Israel and mediated by divine revelation, rather than at the ends of the earth, in mythical lost continents, or in ideal constitutions formulated by political philosophers. In such utopias Israel is constructed as it should have been ("no place") or as it should be in the future ("good place").

The discussion that follows will classify biblical utopias by blending elements of Dawson's outline of classical utopias and Collins's fourfold scheme—not in order to find "influences" of one tradition on the other (although these will be noted if they seem to be present) but for purposes of comparison and contrast. (On the following pages, the term *biblical* will refer both to the Hebrew scriptures and to early Jewish and, in some cases, Christian material inspired by them.) Combining Dawson's and Collins's frameworks, I propose the following classification system:

1. Mythological works, e.g., the Edenic tradition and its biblical and early Jewish developments.
2. Traditions depicting the Land of Israel (or some part of the land) or the nation of Israel in a given historical epoch in idealized terms, subclassified into two genres:
   a. Locative-temporal utopias, that is, traditions in which the land of Israel is portrayed in idealized terms (e.g., the Promised Land, the "land of milk and honey," Jerusalem, the Temple), and periods in the history of Israel as a nation portrayed in the Bible as ideal epochs (e.g., the time of Moses

and Aaron, the kingdoms of David and Solomon, the return from exile). This section will also discuss ideal "maps" of Israel delineated in the Hebrew scriptures.

    b. Legal-covenantal utopias, that is, traditions portraying the Law of Moses founded on the covenant between God and Israel as the supreme template for the ideal theocratic state.

3. Dynamic-theocratic traditions. Based on the explication by Norman Perrin, this is a body of material that understands the world in mythic terms "as being under the direct control of the God who had acted as king on their behalf *and who would continue to do so*,"[6] e.g., traditions of the tribal confederacy (Deut 26:5b-9), royal and enthronement Psalms (Pss 2; 47; 72; 93; 96; 97; 98; 99; 110), and prophecies depicting the restoration of Israel in messianic terms (Isa 11:1-10). The prophets often depict the kingly acts of God to vindicate Israel *in the future* in terms of *idealized past eras*, e.g., as a "new exodus" (Jer 31; 32:40-41; Mal 3:17—4:6), as the "new creation" of Jerusalem (Isa 65:17-25), or as the Temple (Ezekiel 40–48). The kingship/kingdom of God can be portrayed both in particularistic and universalistic terms (e.g., Exod 19:5-6; cf. Deut 7:6; 14:2; 26:18-19).

These utopian expressions seldom exist in pure types, but overlap, blend, and are transformed in the biblical and postbiblical traditions, which may portray Israel simultaneously in both utopian and dystopian terms. In postbiblical times, they find concrete expression in Jewish utopian communities such as the Essenes and the Therapeutai, a phenomenon that will be discussed in the next chapter.

Myths of a Primal Paradise

As Collins notes, "Paradise, or Eden, is the closest biblical approximation to the idea of utopia in its strict sense, *ou topos*, or 'no place.'"[7] Although several book-length studies of the biblical myth of Eden/Paradise have been published,[8] Eden plays a relatively minor role in the Hebrew Bible.[9] The oldest biblical expression of the story appears in Gen 2:4b–3:24, the J (Yahwist) creation account, dated to the tenth century BCE:

> And the LORD GOD planted a garden in Eden, in the east; and there he put the man whom he had formed. Out of the ground the LORD GOD made to grow every tree that is pleasant to the sight and good for food, the tree of life also in the midst of the garden, and the tree of the knowledge of good and evil. A river flows out of Eden to water the garden, and from there it divides and becomes four branches. The name of the first is Pishon; it is the one that flows around the whole land of Havilah, where there is gold; and the gold of that land is good; bdellium and onyx stone are there. The name of the second river is Gihon; it is the one that flows around the whole land of Cush. The name of the third river is Tigris, which flows east of Assyria. And the fourth river is the Euphrates. The LORD GOD took the man and put him in the garden of Eden to till it and keep it. (Gen 2:8-15)

Several derivations have been argued for the Hebrew *'eden*: "steppe or plain" from Sumerian; "pleasure, luxury" from the Hebrew root *'dn*; or the Aramaic *'dn*, "enrich, give abundance."[10] The Septuagint translates the Hebrew phrase *gan 'eden* as *paradeisos tēs tryphēs* (Gen 2:15)—"pleasure-ground of luxury."

The Yahwist creation account is often compared with the ancient Sumerian myth of Dilmun (identified with present-day Bahrain), an island inhabited by gods, a pure land called "the land of the living," where sickness, death, and trouble are unknown:

> In Dilmun the raven uttered no cries,
> The kite uttered not the cry of the kite,
> The lion killed not,
> The wolf snatched not the lamb,
> Unknown was the kid-killing dog.
> (cf. Isa 11:6-7; 65:25; cf. 35:9).[11]

Water is the only thing missing in the garden, and it is quickly supplied by the sun-god Utu at the request of Enki, a water deity; wells of water gush forth from the earth, watering the crops (cf. Gen 2:5-6: "For the LORD GOD had not caused it to rain upon the earth, and there was no one to till the ground; but a stream would rise from the earth, and water the whole face of the ground"). The primal couple in the tale are not human beings, as in the Genesis account, but the god Enki and Ninhursag/Nintu, a mother goddess, who quickly become the progenitors of goddesses (all born without labor pains; cf. Gen 3:16) of vegetation, mountains, and spiders/weaving. The lustful and impulsive god becomes pregnant by greedily ingesting eight plants that sprout from his own semen. Since he is not equipped to give birth, he becomes very ill and must be rescued by Ninhursag, who saves him by placing him in her vagina and giving birth to eight healing goddesses, whose powers correspond to the pains in the god's body. Jean Delumeau notes that while there are similarities between the ancient Mesopotamian and Hebrew myths (the garden, water issuing from beneath the earth, a primal couple, miraculous plants, the eating of "forbidden" vegetation), the salient difference is "the tree of the knowledge of good and evil" (Gen 1:17); disobeying God's command not to eat of its fruit leads to death, prefiguring the theme of covenantal obligation that runs through the Hebrew scriptures.[12]

Terje Stordalen has exhaustively catalogued biblical references to Eden, both overt and covert,[13] distinguishing among Eden similes (e.g., Gen 13:10; Isa 51:3; Ezek 36:35; Joel 2:3), metaphors (e.g., Prov 11:30; Ezek 28:11-19; 47:1-12; Joel 4:18; Zech 14:8-11; Sir 40:27), and allegories (e.g., Eccl 2:1-22; Ezek 28:11-19; 31); as well as allusions and intertextual connections (e.g., Isa 65:17-25; Sir 50:12-13). Passages like Isa 51:3 portray the restoration of God's people to Zion/the Temple in Edenic terms: "For the LORD will comfort Zion; he will comfort all her waste places, and will make *her wilderness like Eden, her desert like the garden of the LORD*" (italics added; cf. Isa 65:25; Ezek 36:35, 47:1-12; Joel 4:18; Zech 14:8). Sapiential writings portray God's Wisdom as the tree of life (e.g., Prov 3:18; 11:30; cf. 13:12; 15:4) or use terminology that evokes the primal garden to laud Wisdom/Torah (Sir 24:25-31; 40:27).

Some early Jewish and Christian writings portray Eden, where the tree of life remains, as the abode of the righteous dead, locating Paradise in any of three possible places:

(1) in a remote location on earth:[14]

> And (I saw) the earth and its fruit. . . . And I saw the garden of Eden and its fruits, and the source and the river flowing from it, and its trees and their flowering, making fruits, and I saw men doing justice in it, their food and their rest (*Apoc. Ab.* 21:3, 6);[15]

(2) in the heavens:[16]

> And he said to me, "If I had asked you, How many dwellings are in the heart of the sea, or how many streams are at the source of the deep, or how many streams are above the firmament, or which are the exits of Hades, *or which are the entrances to paradise?*" Perhaps you would have said to me, "I never went down into the deep, nor as yet into Hades, neither did I ever *ascend into heaven*" (2 Esdr 4:7-8, italics added; cf. 7:36; 8:52);

(3) in an unspecified location:[17]

> And he shall open the gates of paradise; he shall remove the sword that has threatened since Adam, and he will grant to the saints to eat of the tree of life (*Testament of Levi* 18:10).[18]
>
> And he [Jesus] said to him, "Truly I tell you, today you will be with me in Paradise" (Luke 23:43).

These speculations about Eden as the abode of the righteous dead, especially those that locate Paradise in the heavens (cf. 2 Cor 12:2-3), figure prominently in the development of Jewish, Christian, and Muslim beliefs about the afterlife.[19] As Collins notes, certain texts blend the hope of a heavenly paradise with the expectation of a restored land of Israel (e.g., *4 Ezra*; *2 Baruch*; Revelation).[20]

As Collins notes, "Eden is located at the mythical source of all the major rivers of the world in Gen 2:10. . . . Such fantastic geography is exceptional in the biblical tradition."[21] However, there are obvious affinities between the Eden myth and Greek legends of the golden age, the Islands of the Blessed, and utopian realms like Atlantis and the Islands of the Sun. Similarly to the golden age, the perfection of Eden is temporary; the devolution of humankind begins with the first couple and accelerates until the Flood (Genesis 3–8). Plato's myth of Atlantis also recalls this pattern: when the divine admixture in the blood of the Atlanteans becomes diluted, moral and political decline ensues.[22] In the Second Temple period, Eden is interpreted as a realm like the Islands of the Blessed/Elysium, located at the ends of the earth (cf. Panchaïa, Hyperborea, and the Islands of the Sun) or in the heavens (cf. Plutarch, *Moralia* 12).

Israel as Utopia

The Hebrew Bible contains many portrayals of an idealized land of Israel and of periods in the history of the nation remembered as ideal epochs. A related body of tradition represents the Torah, grounded in the covenant between God and Israel, as the supreme template for the ideal state. These materials will be examined under the headings of temporal/locative utopias (idealizations of the land and eras in Israelite history) and legal/covenantal utopias (idealizations of Torah).

TEMPORAL/LOCATIVE UTOPIAS

The phrases "promised land" and "land of milk and honey" have become commonplace expressions denoting longed-for states of bliss, satisfaction, and abundance. In the Bible, God commands Abram/ Abraham to leave his homeland for a new country and promises him "offspring, land, divine guidance, and to become a blessing for the whole world."[23] "Now the LORD said to Abram, 'Go from your country and your kindred and your father's house *to the land I will show you*. I will make of you a great nation, and I will bless you, and make your name great, so that you will be a blessing. I will bless those who bless you, and the one who curses you I will curse; and in you all the families of the earth shall be blessed'" (Gen 12:1-3; italics added). The patriarch migrates to the land of Canaan, which God promises to his descendants as an eternal inheritance (Gen 12:6-7; 13:15-17), a pledge that is later ratified by Abraham's purchase of a field in Machpelah as a burial site for the matriarch Sarah (Gen 23:1-20): "So the field of Ephron in Machpelah, which was to the east of Mamre, the field with the cave that was in it and all the trees that were in the field, throughout its whole area, passed to Abraham as a possession in the presence of the Hittites, in the presence of all who went in at the gate of the city. . . . *The field and the cave that is in it passed from the Hittites into Abraham's possession as a burying place*" (Gen 23:17-18, 20; italics added).

Although the phrase "promised land" is not found in the Bible, the theme of the land as promised to Abraham and his descendants forever is echoed throughout the biblical tradition (e.g., Gen 24:7; 31:13; Exod 13:11; 32:13; Deut 7:8; 11.9; Josh 2:14; 14:9; Jer 11:5; Jdt 5:9; Acts 7:5; Heb 11:9). As W. G. Plaut observes, "We can hardly overemphasize the importance of those biblical passages which, like Gen. 13:15, state that God gave Canaan to Abraham and his offspring forever. From these traditions and memories, amplified by centuries of sacred sentiment, grew a unique relationship between a people and a land."[24] This theme of promise is tempered with the awareness that the land has been taken away from others, a conquest legitimated by vehement assertions of the wickedness of the Canaanites (Deut 9:5; Neh 9:8; Wis 12:3-11; *Jub.* 10:32).[25] Israel's eternal inheritance of the land can be interrupted if the people rebel or behave unjustly (Josh 14:9; 23:15; Neh 9:8; Ps 106:24).

In the exodus and conquest traditions (Exodus-Joshua), the land promised to Israel is repeatedly called a "land oozing with milk and honey" (Exod 3:8, 17; 13:5; 33:3; Lev 20:24; Num 13:28; 14:8; 16:13-14; Deut 6:3; 11:9; 26:9; 27:3; 31:20; Josh 5:6).[26] As Etan Levine notes, in the Bible both milk and honey are represented as delicacies, with many positive symbolic associations:

The Bible abounds with references to milk (or milk products) and honey as luxury items, worthy gifts, articles of
trade, contributions to priests and Levites, and high-energy
foods used by those who camp in the wilderness. Honey
is described as being both healthful and pleasurable, and
literary texts employ it as a metaphor for diverse delights
and benefits such as wisdom, divine guidance, and, along
with milk, sexuality. It is not surprising, therefore, that the
divinely bestowed *manna* in the wilderness has the taste
of honey (Exod 16:31) or that in the future God will deny
sinners milk and honey (Job 20:17). Indeed, as far as food
is concerned, "What is sweeter than honey?"[27]

Levine argues, however, that generations of biblical interpreters have
misconstrued the meaning of the phrase *eretz zavat halav v^ed^evash* by
taking it as referring to the abundant produce of fertile farmlands.
In ancient Palestine, both milk and honey were products of *midbar*
(marginal desert), uncultivated pasturelands where flocks and herds
could graze on wild plants and where wild honey is found "amid the
thickets, bushes and wild flowers."[28] While to a pastoralist a "land of
milk and honey" would appear as a divine gift, to farmers or urbanites,
milk and honey would represent a subsistence diet, even the aftermath
of natural disaster or war (cf. Isa 7:15, 21-22).[29] The wilderness generation, accustomed to shepherding flocks in desert pastures, would have
found the Canaanite "hill country with its lush vegetation of wildflow-
ers, thickets and wild forest . . . perfect for grazing, unrestricted by
agriculture or settlements. Technically speaking, the Promised Land
was, indeed, 'a land oozing milk and honey.'"[30] In the account of the
advance party sent by Moses to survey the land prior to conquest, the
scouts find not only milk and honey in the uncultivated highlands, but
also "fertile valleys, densely populated and farmed, and it was from
there that the scouts had brought back magnificent grape clusters,
pomegranates and figs" (Num 13:23).[31] Although, as Levine notes, the
wooded hills would later be cleared for grazing and settlement (Josh
17:14-15), and there would be ongoing battles with the Canaanites
for the fertile plains,[32] the prophetic literature remembers the land of

Israel in nostalgic, eutopian terms as *eretz zavat halav vᵉdᵉvash* (Jer 11:5; 32:22; Ezek 20:6, 15; Bar 1:20), "the most glorious of all lands" (Ezek 20:6b, 15b). Second Isaiah (Isaiah 40–55) depicts the return from exile as a second exodus from slavery to the "good land."[33]

As noted earlier, Collins locates one strand of utopian biblical tradition in an agrarian vision of Israel, grounded in the Priestly Code of the Pentateuch "with its provision for Levitical cities and a jubilee year when all people should return to their ancestral property." He observes that the goal of such legislation is a sort of "agricultural utopia," as delineated in Lev 26:3-9:

> If you follow my statutes and keep my commandments and observe them faithfully, I will give you your rains in their season, and the land shall yield its produce, and the trees of the field shall yield their fruit. Your threshing shall overtake the vintage, and the vintage shall overtake the sowing; you shall eat your bread to the full, and live securely in your land. And I will grant peace in the land, and you shall lie down, and no one shall make you afraid; I will remove dangerous animals from the land, and no sword shall go through your land. You shall give chase to your enemies, and they shall fall before you by the sword. I will . . . make you fruitful and multiply you; and I will maintain my covenant with you.

Deuteronomy waxes even more poetic on the gift of the land: it is filled with cities, houses, and cisterns that the Israelites did not build, with vineyards and olive groves that the Israelites did not plant (Deut 6:10-11). Unlike Egypt, where the Israelites sowed seed and watered the ground, the new land is watered by the heavens, and "the eyes of the LORD your God are always on it, from the beginning of the year to the end of the year" (Deut 11:12). The depiction of the land in Deut 8:7-10 rivals the mythic realms of the ancient Near Eastern and classical utopias:

> For the LORD your God is bringing you into a good land, a land with flowing streams, with springs and underground

waters welling up in valleys and hills, a land of wheat and barley, of vines and fig trees and pomegranates, a land of olive trees and honey, a land where you may eat bread without scarcity, where you will lack nothing, a lack whose stones are iron and from whose hills you may mine copper. You shall eat your fill and bless the LORD your God for the good land that he has given you.

However, like the golden age and Atlantis, the possession of *eretz hatovah* can be undermined by the moral degradation of its inhabitants (Deut 8:11-20).[34]

Collins locates the background of this utopian vision in ancient Near Eastern mythology. In Ugaritic myth, when Baal escapes from Mot (Death), fat rains down from heaven, and the wadis run with honey.[35] Similarly, in the monarchical period, when most of the population of Israel and Judah worked the land, "the divine blessings were manifested in fertility, by the gift of 'the grain, the wine and the oil' (Hos 2:8), just as they were for Israel's Canaanite neighbors."[36] As Collins observes, the Priestly and Deuteronomic authors blame Israel's failure to achieve utopia on its neglect of covenant law, "with the implication that the ideal society can in principle be brought about by appropriate human behavior."[37] Utopia (the longed-for, divinely ordained national ideal) and dystopia (the often-deplored socio-political reality) exist side by side in the theological imaginations of the biblical authors.

Another stream of utopian imagery in the biblical tradition is grounded in the period of the united monarchy, the rule of David and, especially, Solomon when "Judah and Israel dwelt safely, every man under his vine and under his fig tree, from Dan to Beer-Sheba, all the days of Solomon" (1 Kgs 5:5; cf. Mic 4:4; 1 Macc 4:12).[38] As Shemaryahu Talmon observes, "At that time of unity, Israel experienced unprecedented political and economic advancement. This was also the time when the central Sanctuary dedicated to Israel's God was erected in Jerusalem, the place where biblical monotheism found its clearest cultic expression. This glorious period served as a guiding light for the portrayal of the future."[39] In the exilic era, united Israel, with its legendary kings and glorious Temple, serves as a "primeval

prototype" of an idealized future world.[40] In the utopian realm proclaimed by the prophets, a wise and just king from the line of David
will not only reign in Jerusalem but will serve as a beacon of peace to
all nations (e.g., Isa 9:6-7; 11:1-5, 10; 16:4-5; 32:1-2; Jer 23:5-6; Mic
5:1-4a; cf. Ps 72:2-7; Ezek 37:24-28). The prophets contemporary with
the return from exile under Zerubbabel interpret him as the anointed
one who will restore national fortunes to the monarchical ideal (Zech
3:8; 6:12; Hag 2:22-23): "Peace and salvation will prevail in the land
forever (cf. Hag 2:9; Zech 8:12, 19; 6:13; Mal 2:5 with Isa 52:7; 57:2,
19; 60:17; 66:12 *et al.*). Fields and vineyards will yield their fruits to
the people resettled in their land (cf. Hag 2:15-19; Zech 3:10; 8:12
with Hos 2:23-25; Joel 4:18; Amos 9:13-14 *et al.*, contrasted with Hag
1:3-6, 9-11)."[41]

The apocalyptic *Psalms of Solomon* (first century BCE) vividly portray an ideal future kingdom of Israel ruled by a Davidic monarch:

> See, LORD, and raise up for them their king,
> The son of David, to rule over your servant Israel
> In the time known to you, O God. . . .
> He will gather a holy people
> Whom he will lead in righteousness,
> And he will judge the tribes of the people
> That have been made holy by the LORD their God. . . .
> He will distribute them upon the land according to their
> tribes;
> The alien and the foreigner will no longer live near
> them. . . .
> And he will have gentile nations serving him under his
> yoke, . . .
> And he will purge Jerusalem (and make it) holy as it was
> even from the beginning, . . .
> There will be no unrighteousness among them in his
> days,
> For all shall be holy, and their king shall be the Lord
> Messiah. (17:21-32)[42]

The radical utopian hope of the author is summarized by R. B. Wright:

> When the Messiah appears, he is a kingly figure, a scion of the house of David. As the manifestation of God's kingship over Israel and the world, he overthrows the gentile occupiers, ejects all aliens and sinners, and gathers together a purified nation which he leads in righteousness, justice, and holy wisdom (17:23-25). The dispersed of Israel will return to their homeland (17:31; 11; 8:28); the land will be distributed according to the antique tribal system (17:28); Jerusalem and the Temple will be resanctified (17:30f.). All gentile nations will be subjugated to Israel's king, and Jerusalem and her God will be glorified throughout the world.[43]

While the Pseudo-Solomonic *Psalms* envision the restoration of all Israel to its divinely willed glory, Jerusalem has special status as a holy city, where God's presence in Israel is most intense and where the eschatological ingathering of the people will take place (2:19-21; 8:4; 11:1-9).[44]

As Collins points out, while the "agricultural utopia" tradition survived in the Second Temple period, the utopian aspirations of the time increasingly focused on the transformation of Jerusalem due to the greatly reduced territory of restored Judah.[45] The idyllic oracle of a peaceful kingdom in Isaiah 11:1-9 locates the realm where carnivores and their prey will graze together and children will play with harmless serpents adjacent to God's "holy mountain," Zion (vv. 6-9).[46] As the abode of the Temple, Jerusalem had a special status; the presence of God in the Temple made Mount Zion "the navel of the earth."[47] Collins explains:

> The temple precincts were qualitatively radically different from other space. "Better a day in your courts than a thousand elsewhere" (Ps 84:10). Significantly for our theme, the

holy mountain of God is equated with the garden of Eden
in Ezekiel 28 ("You were in Eden, the garden of God . . .
you were on the holy mountain of God"). The temple, in
effect, was a Paradise which one might visit on pilgrimage
at festival times.[48]

The vision of the new Jerusalem in Ezekiel 40–48 is the "utopian blueprint" for an ideal, eschatological temple-state.[49] The city is embedded
in a consecrated space (*terumah*), extending from the Jordan River to
the Mediterranean Sea, separating the territories of Judah and Benjamin. Within this space, the priests, Levites, city, and prince are assigned
their own strips of land, with the majority of space devoted to the
priests, so that "the city of Jerusalem becomes virtually an appendage
of the temple precinct under the control of the Zadokite priests."[50] Ritual purity would be maintained by restricting Levites and non-Priestly
Israelites to the outer court of the sanctuary; foreigners would be
banned altogether (Ezek 44:9). The city itself would be profane (Ezek
48:15). The Davidic prince would be apolitical; his main function
would be to provide offerings for the Temple sacrifices (Ezek 48:17,
22-25).[51] Other prophets foretell the glory of the future restoration
of the Temple, when "the glory of Lebanon . . . the cypress, the plane,
and the pine" will beautify the temple (Isa 60:13), when the earth, sea
and heavens will be shaken "so that the treasures of all nations would
come in and fill this house with splendor" (Hag 2:6-7).

  As Collins notes, the inclusive expectation of Third Isaiah (Isa
56–66), where the covenant will be extended to all who obey YHWH
(Isa 56:3-8), is fundamentally different from the exclusivistic visions
of Ezekiel and Haggai:

> We have then two distinct kinds of utopian expectation in
> the period of the Judean restoration after the exile, both
> of them locative, in the sense that they are this-worldly
> and rooted specifically in Jerusalem. One is focused on the
> temple and has an intense concern for purity. The other
> favors an open Jerusalem and finds a place for Gentiles in

the new dispensation, even if only in a subordinate role
(Isa 61:5-6).[52]

Collins observes that Diaspora Jews in this period continued to envision the land of Israel, with "Jerusalem as a cosmic center to which people of all races would flock," in eschatological-utopian terms (see *Sib. Or.* 3.744–61; 5.252).[53]

The utopian temple-state of Ezekiel's vision is one of several biblical "maps" of Israel that sketch the ideal contours of the land. In the solemn and numinous covenant ratification ceremony of Gen 15:12-21, God promises Abraham the land "from the river of Egypt to the great river, the river Euphrates, the land of the Kenites, the Kenizzites, the Kadmonites, the Hittites, the Perizzites, the Rephaim, the Amorites, the Canaanites, the Girgashites, and the Jebusites" (Gen 15:18b-21; cf. Exod 23:31; Deut 11:24). In subsequent narratives, the divinely appointed contours of Israel are delineated in detail, with the northern and southern boundaries marked by the cities of Dan and Beersheba (Judg 20:1; 1 Sam 3:20; 2 Sam 3:10; 17:11; 24:2, 15; 1 Kgs 4:25; 2 Chron 30:5).[54] Numbers 34:1–35:15 specifies the borders of the promised land, stipulating how the land will be apportioned among the tribes (cf. Deut 3:12-20), including Levitical cities and cities of refuge. Joshua 13:1–21:25 specifies both the Canaanite territories not yet conquered by Israel (13:1-6) and the geographical allotment of the tribal territories (13:8–21:45), concluding with the notice:

> Thus the LORD gave to Israel all the land that he swore to their ancestors that he would give them; and having taken possession of it, they settled there. And the LORD gave them rest on every side just as he had sworn to their ancestors: not one of all their enemies had withstood them, for the LORD had given all their enemies into their hands. Not one of all the good promises that the LORD had made to the house of Israel had failed; all came to pass. (Josh 21:43-45)

The boundaries are anachronistic and idealizing, probably representing "the extent of the land [actual or perceived] thought to obtain at
the time of David (2 Sam 8:3-14; 1 Kings 8:65)."[55] As the legacy of
divine promise, these boundaries are immutable, perfect, and eternal
from a theological perspective,[56] no matter how imperfect, changeable,
and temporary ancient Israel's historical borders actually were.[57]

The Law as Ideal Constitution

Although obedience to the law of Moses (Torah) is the theological
precondition for Israel to remain in the land in happiness and
prosperity, according to the biblical account, the law was given to
Israel while they were a landless people, encamped at Mount Sinai.
Subsequently, Israel's disobedience to God's commandments prevents
them from entering the land of Canaan for forty years and causes
them to lose the "good land" to foreign empires. The legal corpus
of the Torah, made up of layers of Covenant (Exod 20:22–23:19),
Deuteronomic (Deut 12–26), and Holiness (Lev 17–26) codes, as
Menahem Haran observed, hovers "between utopia and historical
reality."[58] Uffenheimer regards the legal-covenantal tradition as
social-utopian, woven into the fabric of Israelite society.[59] At Sinai,
he asserts, Israel "accepted the Divine commandments and obligations
by an act of free commitment thus creating the utopian counterpart
to any kind of rule based on human force."[60] Both Uffenheimer and
Collins regard the Levitical regulations regarding the sabbatical (Exod
21:2-6; 23:10-11; Deut 15:1-18) and jubilee years (Leviticus 25) as
epitomizing the utopian (or eutopian) character of the law.[61] The
sabbatical laws limit slavery, provide for the remission of debts, and
stipulate an agricultural fallow year in seven-year cycles, reflecting
the weekly rhythm of the Sabbath.[62] Similarly, the jubilee year "begins
in the middle of the seventh sabbatical year (every 49th year) on the
tenth day of the seventh month (the Day of Atonement), and extends,
presumably, into the seventh month of the 50th year, thus overlapping
by just over half a year with the regular Sabbatical year."[63] The jubilee
opens with an impressive nationwide ceremony:

> Then you shall have the trumpet sounded loud; . . . you
> shall have the trumpet sounded throughout your land. And
> you shall hallow the fiftieth year and you shall proclaim
> liberty throughout the land to all its inhabitants. It shall
> be a jubilee for you: you shall return, every one of you, to
> your property and every one of you to your family. That
> fiftieth year shall be a jubilee for you: you shall not sow, or
> reap the aftergrowth, or harvest the unpruned vines. For it
> is a jubilee; it shall be holy to you: you shall eat only what
> the field produces. (Lev 25:9-12)

The laws of jubilee pertain to "the redistribution of real estate, the
cancellation of debts, the freeing of slaves, and the designation of an
agricultural fallow year."[64]

Many scholars see the sabbatical and jubilee legislation as
grounded in a concern for social justice.[65] In a recent article,
Robert S. Kawashima argues that within Priestly worldview, the
"Jubilee Year symbolizes and completes an atonement of socio-
economic pollution,"[66] an observation that also applies to the sabbatical year:[67]

> The Priestly system of thought imagined Israel, at the
> moment of its creation by divine fiat, as an ideal correlation
> of people and land, a sacred order, which, not unlike the
> organization of creation itself as described in the Priestly
> cosmogony of Genesis 1, must periodically be restored.
> Based on this conception of the nation, the priestly legist
> understood slavery and the loss of ancestral land as
> instances of socio-economic pollution, since in both cases
> an Israelite is removed from his proper place in society,
> namely, from family and land. . . . Slavery and the loss of
> land . . . "offend against order" . . . and for this reason, the
> Jubilee Year begins with the proclamation of "liberty" on
> the Day of Atonement, at which point each man returns to
> "his family" and/or "his land" (Lev 25:10, 13, 27, 28, 41). It
> signifies the return of cosmic order to Israel.[68]

Scholars differ as to whether the sabbatical and jubilee legislation were exilic ideals never actually put into practice in ancient Israel (*ou-topos*) or whether they were operative in ancient Israel and later fell into disuse (*eu-topos*).[69] In either case, the jubilee imagery is picked up and amplified by Third Isaiah, who proclaims God's eschatological reign in terms inspired by the Priestly legislation:

> The spirit of the LORD GOD is upon me,
> because the LORD has anointed me;
> he has sent me to bring good news to the oppressed,
> to bind up the brokenhearted,
> to proclaim liberty to the captives, and release to the
>   prisoners,
> to proclaim the year of the Lord's favor, . . .
> to comfort all who mourn. (Isa 61:1-2)[70]

The pseudepigraphal *Book of Jubilees* (second century BCE), pre-occupied with calendrical matters, measures the ages of the earth in cycles of jubilees,[71] with forty-nine jubilees (2,410 years) representing a complete era in world history.[72] The revelations of the book are vouchsafed to Moses on Mount Sinai (*Jub* 1:1-6), at the same time as a new era in world history begins with the giving of the Law (50:1).[73] God reveals to Moses that human life spans have declined through the ages, from nineteen jubilees for the antedeluvian ancients, to fewer than four jubilees for the morally perfect Abraham, to a jubilee and a half (at most) for an "evil generation which sins in the land" (23:14) until the great judgment (23:11).

Jubilees' scheme of the deterioration of the ages of the world is reminiscent of Hesiod's account of the progressive debasement of the eons (cf. Dan 2:31-35). In the last age (contemporary with the time of the author),

> if a man will live a jubilee and a half, they will say about
> him, "He prolonged his life, but the majority of his days
> were suffering and anxiety and affliction. And there was
> no peace, because plague [came] upon plague, and wound
> upon wound, and affliction upon affliction, and evil report

> upon evil report, and sickness upon sickness, and every
> evil judgment of this sort with one another: sickness, and
> downfall, and sleet, and hail, and frost, and fever, and chills,
> and stupor, and famine, and death, and sword, and captiv-
> ity, and all plagues, and suffering." (*Jub.* 23:12-13)[74]

At the end of this evil age, the downward spiral will be reversed from
dystopia to utopia when children begin to study Torah and return
to righteousness (24:26). Life spans will increase to a thousand years
(23:27), and there will be no old age, but only "infants and children"
(23:28): "And all of their days they will be complete and live in peace
and rejoicing and there will be no Satan and no evil (one) who will
destroy, because all of their days will be days of blessing and healing"
(23:29). This restoration of Israel will be effected not by a messiah or
even by direct divine intervention but by human repentance and by
proper observance of the Law.

Hellenized Jewish authors of the first century CE portray Moses
as the consummate lawgiver and the Torah as the ultimate national
constitution. Philo of Alexandria (c. 20 BCE–c. 50 CE) describes Moses
as "the best of all lawgivers in all countries, better in fact than any that
have ever arisen among either the Greeks or the barbarians.... His laws
are most excellent and truly come from God, since they omit nothing
that is needful" (*Life of Moses* 3.12).[75] Since the laws revealed through
Moses are divine, they are "firm, unshaken, immovable, stamped ...
with the seals of nature herself" (3.14); their immutability is dem-
onstrated by the fact that no matter how many upheavals the Jewish
nation has experienced, they have remained constant (3.15). Flavius
Josephus (37–101 CE) portrays Moses as a legislator who surpasses
esteemed lawgivers such as Minos (*Against Apion* 2.161), Lycurgus
(2.225), Solon, and Zaleucus Locrensis (2.154).[76] The laws he delivered
to the Jews exceed the laws of all other nations in antiquity (2.154),
sublimity (2.168–171), and practicality (2.173–174). Unlike other peoples, whose laws are known only to a few, all Jews are continuously
educated in the law through weekly instruction (2.175). Like Philo,
Josephus stresses the faithfulness of the Jewish people to their laws
through "countless calamities" (2. 228), a feat that the highly regarded
Lacedaemonians (Spartans) did not achieve, since they quickly ceased

to be governed by their laws once they lost their liberty and independence (2.227). Jews, in contrast, would rather die than betray their laws, which govern every aspect of their lives (2.232–35).

Dynamic-Theocratic Traditions

As we shall see in chapter 5, the term *theocracy* was first coined by Josephus in order to explain the unique polity of the Jews, who, although dispersed throughout the world, were divinely ruled through the law revealed to Moses (*Against Apion* 2.164–65). However, the idea of divine kingship over Israel is an ancient one. Norman Perrin locates the roots of the symbol of "the kingdom of God" in ancient Near Eastern myth: "In this myth the god had acted as king in creating the world, in the course of which he had overcome and slain the primeval monster. Further, the god continued to act as king by annually renewing the fertility of the earth, and he showed himself to be king of a particular people by sustaining them in their place in the world."[77] This myth was celebrated annually in a new year festival, when the god-king's primeval victory at creation corresponded with spring's triumph over winter.[78]

Like other ancient Near Eastern states, Israel celebrated God's kingship, as illustrated by the "enthronement Psalms" (Psalms 47, 93, 96, 97, 28, 99), punctuated with the confession "YHWH has become king!"[79] This avowal of divine kingship was combined with the distinctively Israelite emphasis on covenant traditions, so that qualities of righteousness, justice, and equity characterize God's rule.[80] The royal-covenantal tradition was also blended with the ancient Hebrew theology of "salvation history" (*Heilsgeschichte*), which celebrates God's activity on behalf of Israel in remembered events: "the migrations of the Patriarchs and the Promise of the Land (Canaan) to them; the Descent into Egypt and prosperity and oppression there; the Deliverance from Egypt at the Exodus; the Red Sea miracle; the Wilderness Wandering; the Giving of the Land (Canaan, the land promised to the Patriarchs)."[81] This melding of the Near Eastern myth, celebrating God's act of creation and world-renewal, and salvation history, recollecting God's activity at key moments in the history of Israel,

Perrin argues, set the stage for the appearance of the "kingdom of God" symbol:[82]

> At the level of language the symbol is derived from the myth of the kingship of God, for *malkuth*, "reign" or "kingdom," is an abstract noun formed from the root *m-l-k,* "reign, be king." At the level of immediate reference, however, the symbol evokes the features of the Salvation History. What happened was that the two myths came together to form one, the myth of God who created the world and is active on behalf of his people in the history of the world, and the symbol evolved to evoke that myth.[83]

The kingdom of God,[84] then, is a dynamic symbol evoking the "mighty power of God, of his kingly activity, of the things which he does in which it becomes manifest that he is indeed king."[85] The myth encompasses God's hand in guiding Israel not only to the promised land but also to Jerusalem, Mount Zion, and the Temple.[86]

For Perrin, myth is a complex of stories that human beings regard as demonstrating the inner meaning of human life and the universe.[87] While Israel remained the people of God in the promised land, the myth of God as beneficent king made sense of Israel's history and place in the world. However, the tumultuous history of Israel and Judah had an impact upon the way the symbol of the kingdom of God was interpreted. The falls of Israel (722 BCE) and Judah (587 BCE) were interpreted by prophets as God's judgment on the kingdoms and their rulers for their disobedience; temporary victories were construed as signs of God's faithfulness to his people. [88] Prophets began to use the old symbolism to express the new hope that God the king would act to deliver his people from the hands of the Assyrians (Israel) or Babylonians (Judah) as he had saved them from slavery in Egypt (e.g., Isa 33:22; 52:7-11). The return from exile under Cyrus the Great (538 BCE) led to exultant prophetic reassertions of the reign of Israel's God (e.g., Isa 45:1-3; Zeph 3:14-15).[89]

The decline in Judea's fortunes under the Ptolemies and Seleucids, and particularly the Roman occupation of 63 BCE, led to more radical reconstruals of the ancient myth that God as king is active on behalf of his chosen people. Apocalyptic works like the *Assumption of Moses* express the myth in increasingly extravagant and supernatural terms:

> And then his [God's] kingdom shall appear throughout
>   his creation,
> And then Satan shall be no more
> And sorrow shall depart with him. . . .
> For the Heavenly One will arise from his royal throne,
> And he will go forth from his holy habitation
> With indignation and wrath on account of his
>   sons. . . .
> For the Most High will arise, the Eternal God alone,
> And he will appear to punish the Gentiles
> Then thou, O Israel, shalt be happy. . . .
> And God will exalt thee,
> And he will cause thee to approach the heaven of the stars.
>   (*Assumption of Moses* 10)[90]

Divine kingship becomes the warrant of the fervent hope that God will act to bring about "a dramatic change in the circumstances of the Jews over against the hated Gentiles,"[91] and that Israel will be exalted to supreme status among the nations. Perrin argues that throughout most of the biblical period, the myth of divine rule functioned as a "tensive symbol," a dynamic, multivalent complex of images and associations whose "meaning could never be exhausted, nor adequately expressed, by any one referent."[92] However, Perrin asserts, in apocalyptic literature, there is a tendency to make the kingdom into a "stenosymbol," a sign that has a simple, one-to-one relationship with that which it symbolizes.[93]

The symbol of divine rule brings a dynamic aspect to the biblical utopian tradition. Rather than idealizing the land of Israel, some era in the history of the nation, or the law as ideal constitution, the symbol evokes God-the-king's activity among the people, in the land of Israel and in the cosmos:

Even the sparrow finds a home,
and the swallow a nest for herself,
where she may lay her young,
at your altars, O Lord of hosts,
my King and my God. (Ps 84:3)

The Lord is king forever and ever;
the nations shall perish from his land. (Ps 10:16)

Who is the King of glory?
The Lord, strong and mighty,
the Lord, mighty in battle. (Ps 24:8)

For the Lord, the Most High, is awesome,
a great king over all the earth.
He subdued peoples under us,
and nations under our feet.
He chose our heritage for us,
the pride of Jacob whom he loves. (Ps 47:2-4)

The Lord sits enthroned over the flood;
the Lord sits enthroned as king forever. (Ps 29:10)

For the Lord is a great God,
And a great King above all gods.
In his hand are the depths of the earth;
the heights of the mountains are his also.
The sea is his, for he made it,
and the dry land, which his hands have formed.
(Ps 95:3-5)[94]

While grounded in ancient Near Eastern myth, the distinctively
Israelite-Jewish perspective integrates salvation history and covenant
with the theme of God's dominion over the cosmos: "Now therefore,
if you obey my voice and keep my covenant, *you shall be my treasured*

possession out of all the peoples. Indeed, *the whole earth is mine,* but you shall be for me *a priestly kingdom and a holy nation*" (Exod 19:5-6, italics added; cf. Deut 7:6; 14:2; 26:18-19). Unlike Josephus's concept of theocracy (more accurately, *nomocracy*), which emphasizes the instrumentality of the law in the exercise of divine rule, the myth evoked in these psalms imagines both Israel and the world under the ideal regime par excellence: the kingdom of God.

IDEAL COMMUNITIES *in* EARLY JUDAISM: ESSENES, THERAPEUTAI, *HAVURAH*

3

As discussed in chapter 1, the evidence for the foundation of actual utopian communities is scanty in the Greek tradition.[1] In fact, the two best-attested examples of ancient utopian communities are Jewish: the Essenes, mentioned by both Philo and Josephus, and the Therapeutai, a group of monastic sectarians described by Philo.[2] Arguably, both the Essenes and the Therapeutai were influenced by hellenistic utopian ideas. Even more likely, both Philo and Josephus shaped their accounts of the sectarians in accordance with the conventions of hellenistic utopian literature. Jacob Neusner, a contemporary scholar, describes another ancient Jewish fellowship, the Pharisaic *havurah*,[3] as utopian; the *havurah* will be briefly discussed at the end of this chapter.

The Essenes

The primary sources for the Essenes are Philo, Josephus, and Pliny the Elder. Many scholars also regard the Dead Sea Scrolls as Essene documents, although this identification is hotly disputed.[4] Here, the Essene hypothesis will be accepted with some caution.[5]

The accounts of the Essenes in the ancient sources are somewhat contradictory. According to Pliny's brief report, written late in the first century CE (*Natural History* 5.17.4), the Essenes were located west of the Dead Sea, at a distance from the shore. He alludes to their great antiquity and refers to them as a nation or race. He describes them as highly ethical, eschewing women and money; they maintained their numbers by accepting new men into the community.

Philo (*That Every Good Person Is Free* 72–91; *Hypothetica* 1–18) is the earliest author to use the term *Essene,* which he etymologizes as referring to their holiness, based on the Greek term *hosiotēs.* According to Philo, the sect placed a high value on sanctity but did not offer animal sacrifices. Originating in Palestine, they were village-dwellers,[6] with a population of more than four thousand supported primarily by agriculture and craftwork. They shared possessions, scorned commerce, pooled any wages they earned, dined communally, shared clothing, were pacifists, had no slaves, and rejected marriage and children. They lived without luxuries and wore simple garments, consisting of "stout coats" in winter and "cheap vests" in summer (*Hypothetica* 11.12). Elders were cared for by the younger members of the community as children care for their parents. Their philosophical education consisted of instruction in the ancestral laws.

Josephus, who claims to have participated in the Essene life for a time (*Life* 1.2.10–12), also refers to the sect in *Jewish War* (2.8, 2–13, 119–61) and *Jewish Antiquities* (18.1, 2, 5, 11, 18–22). Like Philo and Pliny, he locates their origins in Palestine, stating that they lived in various towns throughout the land. Their way of life, customs, and laws were similar to those of other Jews, but unlike other Jews they rejected marriage and slavery.[7] Josephus describes their daily routine in some detail: they awake before sunrise to work at tasks assigned by their governors; at the fifth hour they don white veils and partake in ritual baths. Next, they share a simple, common meal, praising God before and after dining. Their sabbath observance is extremely strict (*War* 2.145). Their lives are completely directed by the leaders of the community. They avoid oaths, and they study the ancient scriptures and the uses of roots and stones for medicinal purposes (*War* 2.135). Because of their simplicity of life, they are long-lived, with many reaching the age of one hundred (*War* 2.150). Josephus describes the initiation process for new members in some detail: a postulant must remain outside the sect for a year, after which he is given a digging tool, a girdle, and a white garment. On entering, he learns to conform to the Essene way of life and participates in the baths of purification, but he is still not a full member. His character is further tested for two years; if he measures up, he is allowed to enter the community permanently (*War* 2.137, 150). Some Essenes have prophetic powers (2.159), and all believe in the immortality of the soul (11.154), a doctrine that Josephus compares to the Greek notion of the Islands of the Blessed.

If, as most scholars hold, the Dead Sea Scrolls are indeed Essene documents, they give a more detailed, firsthand account of sectarian beliefs than the hellenistic authors; however, it must be noted that this identification is not certain. As Collins observes, the Qumran Temple Scroll (11Q19–20) and the fragmentary Vision of the New Jerusalem (4Q544) represent "the purist strand in Jewish utopian thought" to an extreme.[8] He describes the latter in some detail:

> Clearly modeled on the vision of Ezekiel, the text is narrated in the first person by a visionary who is given a guided tour by an angel. In contrast to Ezekiel's vision, the temple is located within the city, which is envisioned as an immense rectangle. It is divided by six large avenues linking the twelve gates and forming sixteen big blocks of houses. One of these avenues runs through the center of the city, and so the temple is slightly off-center. It is likely that the New Jerusalem text was influenced by Hellenistic city planning, even at the expense of the perfect symmetry that we find in the Temple Scroll.[9]

As in Ezekiel's vision of the New Jerusalem, the buildings in the city are made of precious stones. The temple in the New Jerusalem is an eschatological temple, divinely created.[10]

Collins observes that the Temple Scroll, based on the laws in Leviticus and Deuteronomy, "may reasonably be considered a utopian document in the sense that it is a blueprint for an ideal society."[11] The new temple is envisioned as about three times larger than the Herodian structure and is characterized by extreme purity and strict legal observance. Although reminiscent of Ezekiel 40–48, unlike Ezekiel the Temple Scroll describes the city as partaking in the holiness of the temple.[12] The city is so pure that its latrine must be at least three thousand cubits outside the walls, and a man may not enter the city for three days after having sexual relations with his wife.[13] The temple is located in the center of the city, which is in the center of the land. Three concentric courtyards surround the temple: one reserved for priests, one for Israelite men over twenty, and a third for Israelite women and foreigners born in the land of Israel.[14] The lands allotted to the tribes are arranged around the city so that all have equal access (cf. Exod 25:8).[15] Collins argues that while the Temple Scroll epitomizes the vision of utopia "in terms of the sanctity of the temple and the temple city" initiated by Ezekiel, the city and temple of the Scroll are not eschatological: "The king in the Scroll is not said to fulfill messianic prophecy and his rule is conditional. The Scroll is certainly utopian in character, in the sense that it is incongruous with the state of reality in which it occurs, but it stops short of the definitive claims characteristic of apocalyptic visions."[16]

The Dead Sea sect's utopian dream of an ideal temple in a new Jerusalem arose out of their disdain for the impurity of the actual temple and city. Their own community was envisioned as "an everlasting plantation, a house of holiness for Israel, an assembly of supreme holiness for Aaron . . . a Most Holy Dwelling for Aaron, with everlasting knowledge of the covenant of justice, and it shall offer up sweet fragrance. . . . And they shall be an agreeable offering, atoning for the Land and determining the judgment of wickedness, and there shall be no more iniquity" (1QS 8:5–10).[17] The charter of the sect is found in 1QS 8:13–14 (the *Community Rule*): "separate from the habitation of unjust men and go into the wilderness to prepare there the way of Him, as it is written, *Prepare in the wilderness the way of . . . make straight in the Desert a path for our God.*[18] Estranged from the real-life Temple, the sectarians founded an idealized temple-community in the desert, regulated by a strict code of conduct (the Rule), anticipating the day when a new, purified temple, city, and land would be established. The *yahad* (the term used in the Dead Sea Scrolls for the community) was conceived metaphorically as a sacrifice, atoning for the unholiness of the offerings in the real Temple.

The similarities between some of the hellenistic utopias, especially the romances and ideal constitutions discussed in chapter 2, and the Essenes as described by Pliny, Philo, and Josephus are patent.[19] Doron Mendels has gone so far as to argue that the primary template for the Essenes in their attempt to create an ideal Jewish society was the hellenistic utopia, particularly Iambulus's Islands of the Sun (Diodorus Siculus 2.55–60), "fleshed out with a Jewish theology which was influenced by a pagan environment."[20] Mendels adduces an impressive list of parallels between the Essenes and the Heliopolitans: location in isolated areas; distinctive "national identities"; emphasis on internal harmony; leadership of elders; no private property; common meals; asceticism; uniformity of dress; natural derivation of subsistence; ritual baths; rejection of marriage; communal child rearing; rejection of temple worship; simple burial system; dualistic worldview; association of the deity with the sun; love of learning, especially astrology; cryptic writings; special skill in healing.[21] Mendels argues that all of these parallels are supported not just by the descriptions in Philo and Josephus but also by references in the Scrolls;[22] consequently, the resemblance is more than the construction of the Essenes in utopian terms by hellenized Jews for a pagan audience.[23] At the very least, the idea that the Jewish authors presented the Essenes using utopian motifs familiar to their Greek-speaking audiences is appealing.

Both Philo and Josephus show an awareness of the genre of the hellenistic utopia. As noted earlier, in *War* (2.155–156), Josephus refers to the Essene belief that good souls find their final reward in a realm "beyond the ocean, a place which is not oppressed by rain or snow or heat, but is refreshed by the ever gentle breath of the west wind coming in from the ocean. . . . The Greeks, I imagine, had the same conception when they set apart the isles of the blessed for their brave men, whom they call heroes and demigods."[24] In *Against Apion* (2.220–24), Josephus argues that the Jewish nation and its laws are so extraordinary that if "some one had delivered a lecture to the Greeks which he admitted to be the outcome of his own imagination, or asserted that somewhere outside the known world he had met with people who held such sublime ideas about God and had for ages continued steadily faithful to such laws as ours; his words would, I imagine, astonish all his hearers, in view of the constant vicissitudes in their own past history" (221).[25] He goes on to refer to Greek writers who have composed accounts of ideal societies and are accused of writing tales of wonder (*thaumasta*) impossible to implement (222). That is, a Gentile who did not know of the actual existence of the Jews would mistake a *truthful* description of their way of life for a hellenistic utopian fantasy or a philosopher's dream of an ideal state (cf. *Against Apion* 2.222b–223).

The Therapeutai/Therapeutrides

Another Jewish utopian community, located near Lake Mareotis in Egypt, was the Therapeutai/Therapeutrides,[26] described by Philo in *On the Contemplative Life*. This sect, Philo attests, like the Essenes in Judaea, lived a common life, devoid of personal possessions. Most scholars have assumed that Philo's account is of an actual (although perhaps somewhat idealized) monastic order that dwelt near Alexandria in Philo's time.[27] In a recent article, however, Troels Engberg-Pedersen makes an interesting case that Philo's account is not a description of a historical Jewish community but rather a "philosopher's dream," a fictional story (*plasma*) written for the serious purpose of illustrating the life of *theōria* or contemplation (*Life* 1).[28] Engberg-Pedersen admits that Philo might have known of a coventicle remotely like the Therapeutai in the vicinity of Alexandria, but asserts that it doesn't matter much "whether there were people *a little bit* like Philo's Therapeutai or not," since methodologically, it is impossible to choose between the suggestion that Philo's description is "fairly extensively idealized" and the supposition that it is all fiction.[29] For Engberg-Pedersen, Philo's *Contemplative Life* belongs to the ancient genre of fictional accounts of the ideal society (e.g., Plato's *Republic*, Zeno's *Republic*), which by Philo's time had been jumbled together generically with fantastic travel narratives (e.g., the marvelous tales in Herodotus, the Hyperboreans of Hecateaus of Abdera, Euhemerus of Messene's *Sacred Inscription*).[30] Engberg-Pedersen offers slighting references to literary accounts of ideal societies in Lucian of Samosata and Josephus as evidence that in Graeco-Roman times, the genre (whether philosophical or fantastic) had fallen into disrepute (Lucian, *True History* 1.1–4; Josephus, *Against Apion* 2.220–224).[31] Philo wanted to describe an ideal Jewish society, argues Engberg-Pedersen, but he did not want to invite incredulity by presenting the account as his own creation, or to dissociate it from Judaism by placing it outside the boundaries of the known world. Therefore, he chose "to present his ideal state as a historical fact . . . *without* admitting its fictitious character . . . and to locate it *within* the confines of the known world."[32]

While Engberg-Pedersen's hypothesis is intriguing and his case vigorously argued, he does not adequately address three aspects of Philo's presentation of the Therapeutai that point to the historical reality of the Egyptian Jewish contemplatives. First, Philo begins his treatise with a reference to a previous discussion of the Essenes (*Life* 1), who are offered as an ideal example of the active life (*praktikon bion*).[33] Whether Philo's reference to the Essenes refers to his discussion in *That Every Good Person Is Free* (75–87), the *Hypothetica* (11.1–18), or a third, no longer extant account,[34] there is no doubting the historical reality of the Essenes, attested to by both Pliny and Josephus and widely identified with the writers of the Dead Sea Scrolls. Philo's prior use of the Essenes as an example of the *active* life leads the reader to expect that his account of the *contemplative* life will also draw on a real-life example, the Therapeutai/Therapeutrides (*Life* 2), a class of philosophers who exist "in many places in the inhabited world" (*Life* 21), but the best of whom are an Egyptian Jewish sect known to the author (*Life* 22).[35]

Second, Philo begins his treatise with a strong statement of his commitment to conveying the actual truth (*autēs . . . tēs alētheias; Life* 1); Engberg-Pedersen's assertion that the emphatic truth claim was meant to conceal the fact that the Therapeutai were nonexistent seems overly ingenious.[36] Third, Philo gives a fairly detailed account of the location of this sect, "situated above the Mareotic Lake on a somewhat low-lying hill very happily placed both because of its security and the pleasantly tempered air" (*Life* 23).[37] Engberg-Pedersen argues that Philo refrained from revealing the fact that the Therapeutai were his own invention in order to avoid the criticism that his account of the ideal state was based on "impossible premises,"[38] but the observable geographical fact that no such community dwelt on the shores of Lake Mareotis in his time would have been much more damaging to Philo's case. Therefore, Taylor and Davies's theory that the community of Therapeutai was "very small and composed of certain people from an affluent, educated circle in Alexandria, a circle in which Philo himself participated," and who followed a lifestyle distinct from that of the Essenes in Judea, seems more plausible than the suggestion that they were a philosophical fantasy.[39]

Although Engberg-Pedersen's hypothesis is not altogether persuasive, the suggestion that there is a relationship between ancient fictional accounts of ideal societies and Philo's *Life* invites further investigation. Philo insists that his narrative will not "add anything of my own procuring to improve upon the facts as is constantly done by poets [*poiētais*] and historians [*logographois*] through lack of excellence in the lives and practices which they record" (*Life* 1.1). He continues by asserting that the virtue of the philosophers he is about to describe is enough to unnerve the greatest orator, but that such excellence must not go unrecorded. Like Josephus in *Against Apion*, Philo compares the *actual* lives of Jews (in this case, the Therapeutai and Therapeutrides) with the exaggerated accounts of poets and romance writers.[40] If, as I argue below, Philo's account *resembles* the fantastic tales of poets and historians, this is because (as Philo might have argued) the reality of these Jewish philosophers was so superlative that others might mistake it for invention. In particular, Philo's description of the (real-life) sect echoes the kinds of hellenistic romances described in chapter 2, with particular reference to Iambulus's tale of the Islands of the Sun.[41]

Similarities between the Therapeutai and the Heliopolitans

Iambulus's account of the Islands of the Sun, as mentioned earlier, is preserved fragmentarily in Diodorus Siculus 2.55–59.[42] Superficially, Philo's relatively sober and realistic description of the Therapeutai seems far removed from Iambulus's marvelous tale of the Heliopolitans. However, on closer inspection, the Therapeutai and the islanders share a long list of similarities:

1. *Location and climate.* Both are located in isolated areas: the Heliopolitans on their remote islands (Diodorus 2.55.6); the Therapeutai in general "outside the walls pursuing solitude in gardens or lonely bits of country" (*Life* 20). The Egyptian Jewish ascetics in particular reside in a place "secured by the farm buildings and villages round about" (*Life* 23a). Both enjoy salubrious climates (Diodorus 2.56.7; *Life* 23).

2. *Simple, natural diet.* The Therapeutai eat an extremely simple and pure diet of bread, salt, and hyssop with spring water to drink (*Life* 37a, 73–74, 81–82). The Heliopolitans differ from the Therapeutai in that they do eat meat and drink wine, which their islands spontaneously produce in abundance (Diodorus 2.59.2–3). However, both groups eat simple, natural foods, unaccompanied by elaborate sauces or condiments (Diodorus 2.59.1, 5; the salt and hyssop eaten with the bread of the Therapeutai have ritual connotations; cf. *Life* 81–82). Both groups practice restraint in their eating habits:

   > Although all the inhabitants enjoy an abundant provision of everything from what grows of itself in these islands, yet they do not indulge in the enjoyment of this abundance without restraint, but they practice

simplicity and take for their food only what suffices for
their needs. (Diodorus 2.59.1)

> For as nature has set hunger and thirst as mis-
> tresses over mortal kind they propitiate them without
> using anything to curry favor but only such things as
> are actually needed and without which life cannot be
> maintained. Therefore they eat enough to keep from
> hunger and drink enough to keep from thirst but abhor
> surfeiting as a malignant enemy both to soul and body.
> (*Life* 37)

3. *Uniformity of dress.* Members of both communities wear simple
   clothing. The Therapeutai wear "a thick coat of shaggy skin"
   in winter and "a vest or linen shirt" in summer (*Life* 38); at
   their communal banquets, however, they all dress in white
   (*Life* 87). The Heliopolitans make their clothing from a native
   reed, whose fibers are mingled with crushed seashells to create
   "remarkable garments of a purple hue" (Diodorus 2.49.4a).

4. *Rejection of marriage/communal child rearing.* The Heliopolitans
   do not marry, and they practice communal child rearing (*hōs
   koinous*; Diodorus 2.58.1). The Therapeutai divest themselves
   of possessions and leave behind their families, friends, and
   homelands (*Life* 18). Among them are "aged [female] virgins"
   who have voluntarily eschewed marriage in favor of the pursuit
   of wisdom (*Life* 68). According to Philo, the (widowed male?)
   Therapeutai leave their biological offspring behind, while the
   women "desire no moral offspring but those immortal children
   which only the soul that is dear to God can bring to the birth
   unaided because the father has sown in her spiritual rays" (*Life*
   68). The younger Therapeutai treat the elder men and women
   like fathers and mothers, "judging them to be the parents of
   them all in common [*koinous autōn goneis*], in a closer affinity
   than that of blood, since to the right minded there is no closer
   tie than noble living" (*Life* 72).

5. *Testing of children/neophytes.* The children of the Heliopolitans are subjected to a life-threatening initiation that tests their

spiritual worthiness and determines whether they will survive or perish (Diodorus 2.58.5). The Therapeutai only admit those junior members who are "chosen on merit with all care who as becomes their good character and nobility [*eugeneis*] are pressing on to reach the summit of virtue" (*Life* 72). The juniors among the Therapeutai are not necessarily chronologically young but those who have recently been admitted to the community (*Life* 67).

6. *Dining habits.* Philo's description implies that the Therapeutai normally dine separately, after sunset (*Life* 34); some are so disciplined that they eat only after three or even six days (*Life* 33–34). They eat communally every seven days (*Life* 37) and at a festival celebrated "after seven sets of seven days" (*Life* 65). The Heliopolitans—unlike many other ancient utopians—"do not all take their food at the same time nor is it always the same" (Diodorus 2.59.5); unlike the Therapeutai, there is no mention of meals associated with their festivals (2.59.7).

7. *Leadership by elders.* Each clan of the Heliopolitans is led by an elder (*presbyteros*), who is universally obeyed (Diodorus 2.58.6); similarly, the Therapeutai are taught by the senior (*presbyteros*) among them at their weekly assemblies, where they listen to him with great attention (*Life* 31). The neophytes wait on the elder men and women (*Life* 67–68).

8. *Love of learning.* The Heliopolitans are described as attending to "every branch of learning and especially to astrology" (Diodorus 2.57.4). The Therapeutai spend their days closeted with "laws and oracles delivered through the mouth of prophets, and psalms and anything else which fosters and perfects knowledge and piety" (*Life* 25). Scriptural reading and allegorical interpretation are an important element in their spiritual pursuits (*Life* 28–29).

9. *Association with healing.* Philo explains the term *therapeutai/ therapetrides* as denoting "an art of healing better than that current in the cities which cures only the bodies, while theirs treats also souls oppressed with grievous and well-nigh incurable diseases, inflicted by pleasures and desires and griefs

and fears" (*Life* 2–3).[43] The islands of the sun are home to a species of animals whose blood has miraculous bodily healing properties (Diodorus 2.58.4); the island waters also have medicinal qualities, "the warm springs serving well for bathing and the relief of fatigue, the cold excellent in sweetness and possessing the power to contribute to good health" (Diodorus 2.57.3). Healing of the soul is not mentioned with respect to the children of the sun, presumably because it is not required in an ideal society.

10. *Physical peculiarities.* The Heliopolitans are described as being physically very different from other people (Diodorus 2.55.2–6). While the Therapeutai are not described as having notable physical peculiarities, Philo says that the most rigorous devotees "have become habituated to abstinence like the grasshoppers who are said to live on air" (*Life* 35); that is, through self-discipline they have become physically unlike the majority of humankind.

11. *Absence of slavery.* The topic of slavery is not explicitly addressed by Iambulus, but it is evident that there are no slaves among the Heliopolitans, who "take turns in ministering to the needs of one another, some of them fishing, others working at the crafts, others occupying themselves in other useful tasks, and still others, with the exception of those who have come to old age, performing the services of the group in a definite cycle" (Diodorus 2.59.6–7). According to Philo, the Therapeutai repudiate slavery "as they consider the ownership of servants to be entirely against nature" (*Life* 70a; cf. 71). Philo mentions that the junior members of the community wait on the elders at their sacred banquets (*Life* 72). Taylor and Davies surmise that the neophytes played a key role in the economic life of the Therapeutai and in supporting the elders in their spiritual endeavors.[44]

12. *Association of the divine with the sun.* The Heliopolitans "worship as gods that which encompasses all things and the sun, and in general all the heavenly bodies" (Diodorus 2.59.2); they sing "especially in honor of the sun, after whom they name

both the islands and themselves" (2.59.7). Of course, the Jewish ascetics know better than to worship the sun or the heavenly bodies (*Life* 5), but each day they pray at dawn and at sunset (*Life* 27), and philosophize only during the daylight hours, since this is work worthy of the light (*Life* 34). At the close of their forty-ninth-day banquets, "they stand with their faces and their whole bodies turned to the east and when they see the sun rising they stretch their hand up to heaven and pray for bright days and knowledge of the truth and the power of keen sighted thinking" (*Life* 89).

13. *Hymn singing.* The Heliopolitans both pronounce and sing "hymns and spoken laudations" in honor of their deities, especially the sun (Diodorus 2.59.7). Philo gives a lengthy description of the choral singing and dancing of the Therapeutai and Therapeutrides at their forty-ninth-day banquets (*Life* 83–89).

14. *Numerical symbolism.* There are seven Islands of the Sun (Diodorus 2.58.7b); the Heliopolitans' alphabet consists of seven letters, each of which can be formed in four distinct ways (2.57.4); Iambulus is expelled from the Islands after seven years (2.60.1). The maximum lifespan allowed to the islanders, 150 years (2.57.5), is, of course, three times *fifty*, called by Philo "the most sacred of numbers and the most deeply rooted in nature, being formed from the square of the right-angled triangle which is the source from which the universe springs" (*Life* 65). The Therapeutai venerate both the seventh day, "as one of perfect holiness and a most complete festival" (*Life* 36), and the sabbath of weeks, "venerating not only the simple week of seven days, but also its multiplied power, for they know it to be pure and always virgin," celebrating their most sacred rites on the eve of the fiftieth day (*Life* 65).

15. *Love of harmony.* The Heliopolitans are free of rivalry, "and they never cease placing the highest value on internal harmony" (*tēn homonoian*; Diodorus 2.58.1b). Philo emphasizes the musical and social harmony of the Therapeutai at their great banquets *antiphōnois harmoniais*; *enarmonion symphōnian*; *Life* 84, 88).

16. *Simplicity and self-control.* As noted above, the Heliopolitans practice restraint and discipline in their eating habits, child-rearing practices, method of government, and rotation of labor. Children and adults who are less than perfect are euthanized (Diodorus 2.57.5; 2.58.5). According to Philo, self-control (*engkrateian*) and simplicity (*atyphian*) are foundational values among the Therapeutai (*Life* 34, 39).

17. *Blessed existence.* Iambulus and his companion are sent by the Ethiopians to find a land where they would lead a "blessed life" (*par' hois makariōs zēsetai*; Diodorus 2.55.4); Philo describes the Therapeutai as desiring "a deathless and blessed life" (*athanatou kai makarias zōēs*; *Life* 13), and as citizens of heaven and of the world (*ouranou . . . kai kosmou politōn*; *Life* 90).

Differences between the Therapeutai and the Heliopolitans

Of course, there are significant differences between the Jewish sectarians and the children of the sun. The Therapeutai live near Philo's metropolis of Alexandria, whereas the islands of the Heliopolitans are so remote that different constellations appear in their night sky. The Therapeutai are (for the most part) physically indistinguishable from other human beings, whereas the Heliopolitans have distinctive bodily characteristics. Strange animals and plants with miraculous properties inhabit the islands; Philo describes no such marvels among the Therapeutai. The infant children of the Islanders are required to mount the backs of giant birds to prove their worthiness to live, whereas neophytes are admitted by the Therapeutai on the basis of their lofty aspirations. The Heliopolitans self-euthanize at an advanced age and are buried in a simple manner; Philo does not mention the death-rites of the Therapeutai. The "children" inhabit seven islands, which are their native home, and live in clans of four hundred members, whereas the Therapeutai are a small, identifiably Jewish sectarian community who choose to leave family and friends behind—or, in the case of the women, eschew them altogether—in order to pursue the *vita contemplativa*. The Heliopolitans spend their days working to provide for the needs of their people; the Therapeutai are ascetics who spend their time in solitary study and meditation, communing only at their sabbaths and pentecosts. Possibly, as Taylor and Davies argue, their economic needs were attended to by the younger members of the community.

Many of the differences between the Therapeutai and the children of the sun can be explained by the difference in genre between Iambulus's and Philo's narratives. While the Heliopolitans are, indeed, the figments of the imagination of the kind of writer criticized by Philo at the beginning of his treatise (*Life* 1), the Therapeutai are an actual community known to him. Because the Therapeutai actually exist, and because he has personal knowledge of them, Philo describes them in a truthful manner (*autēs . . . tēs alētheias*; *Life* 1), that is, without the kinds of fantastic details characteristic of hellenistic utopists like Iambulus (e.g., giant birds, miraculous animals, superhuman inhabitants). Perhaps because Philo regarded the Therapeutai similarly to the way that Josephus viewed the Jews in general (*Against Apion* 2.220–24), as a community whose actual way of life was so sublime that a Greek reader would hear it with wonder (*thaumasai*) as a marvelous tale (*thaumasta*), his description of them includes hellenistic utopian *topoi* that would be recognized by his educated Alexandrian audience, including members of the Therapeutai. Possibly, the Alexandrian Therapeutic sect was deliberately founded on hellenistic utopian principles, although the paucity of evidence about them would make this difficult to establish.[45]

Thus, contrary to Engberg-Pedersen's assertion that it is methodologically impossible to decide whether Philo's account of the Therapeutai is idealized fact or purely a "philosopher's dream,"[46] there are good reasons to conclude that the former is the case. The Therapeutai, like the Essenes, were an actual group of Jewish ascetics known to Philo. They lived in a specific geographical area explicitly described by Philo, which easily could have been checked by his readers. Philo's description of them deliberately accentuates the similarities between the "blessed lives" of the Therapeutai and those of imaginary ideal societies like the Heliopolitans, but it is realistic enough to justify his assertion that his narrative is true.[47] Rather than being a philosopher's dream, Philo's account of the Therapeutai is a utopian construction of a real (*alētheian*) community.

The Pharisaic Havurah

Both the Essenes and the Therapeutai/Therapeutrides observed Torah far more meticulously than the majority of their Jewish contemporaries. Another ancient Jewish group that scrupulously obeyed the law was the Pharisees. However, unlike the other sectarians, the Pharisees searched "for the godly community within the society of men."[48] The distinguished scholar of Judaism Jacob Neusner has called the Pharisaic *havurah* (based on the Hebrew word for "friend," *haver*) a "road to Utopia" alternative to the separatism of the Essenes (or the Therapeutai).[49] As described by Neusner, the *havurah* was "distinguished . . . from the common people by observing even the most neglected details of the Torah, the laws of ritual purity . . . and giving tithes and heave-offerings as set forth in Scripture. In doing so, they cast up a barrier between themselves and the outsider (called in the sources the *am ha-aretz*), for an outsider was for many reasons a potential source of ritual defilement."[50]

Neusner asserts that, although members of the *havurah* did not separate themselves spatially from other Jews in the sense of living in separate communities, within their hometowns and villages ("within them but not of them"),[51] they formed a "separate society," grounded in the conviction that "all Israel is to be a kingdom of priests and a holy people (and this was understood to mean at the very least a people ritually pure and holy), and second, that every individual Jew everywhere was himself to be as ritually fit as a priest to perform the sacrificial act in the Temple."[52] By their example and teachings, members of the *havurah* endeavored both to transform and to transcend society, "to live Utopia in an unredeemed world."[53]

This way of life was open to any willing Jew, irrespective of age, class, or gender:

> Wives might join without their husbands, and children without their parents, although if they were born to a family known to adhere to the rule, they were assumed to be observant until they gave evidence to the contrary. The fellowship cut across caste lines as well, for some members of the priestly and Levitical castes were associates and others were not. . . . A slave might become an associate without his master and vice versa.[54]

Neusner identifies three "stages of affiliation" marking entry into the *havurah*: the giving of all scripturally stipulated tithes and heave-offerings (the part of a peace-offering dedicated to the priests); the commitment to ensure the ritual purity of these sacrifices and to eat *all* food in a state of ritual purity; and, finally, the promise to guard all foods from defilement, both within and outside the home.[55]

Scholars differ as to whether only a select group of Pharisees considered themselves to belong to the *havurah*, or whether *haverim* ("friends") was simply the name the Pharisees used for themselves. Jacob Neusner and Aharon Oppenheimer take the former position;[56] Tal Ilan takes the latter.[57] The term *Pharisees* (*perushim*, "separatists") is a derogatory term in the rabbinic literature, usually put on the lips of their opponents.[58] Neusner and Oppenheimer assume that since the rabbis distinguish between the *perushim* and the *haverim*, the two must have been distinct, with the latter being a subgroup of the former. Ilan, however, argues that the Tosefta distinguishes between the *am ha-aretz* ("people of the land," ordinary Jews) and the *havurah* in sectarian terms, making no distinction between Pharisees and *haverim*.[59] The rabbis of the Mishnah also characterize themselves as *haverim*, but without the sectarian bias of the Tosefta. In the Mishnah the rabbis are "companions," and the *am ha-aretz* are simply nonobservant Jews; whereas in Tosefta, the *havurah* is a distinctive sect, and the "people of the land" are nonsectarian Jews.

Whether only a select group of Pharisees belonged to the *havurah*, or all Pharisees regarded one another as *haverim*, the existence of a sectarian table-fellowship that bore witness to its strict interpretation of Torah while remaining active in urban life exemplifies an approach to the practice of an ideal Jewish way of life distinctive from the more literally separatist Essenes and Therapeutai. Apart from its intrinsic interest, the Pharisaic *havurah* provides an intriguing parallel with the kingdom of God movement whose disciples carried out their mission within society while belonging to an invisible divine commonwealth.

JESUS *and the* KINGDOM *of* GOD *in* BIBLICAL SCHOLARSHIP

There is a broad consensus among biblical scholars that the kingdom of God (*hē basileia tou theou*) was central to Jesus' preaching.[1] This is not matched by agreement as to the significance of the phrase for Jesus. This chapter[2] will provide an overview of the main lines of research on Jesus' proclamation of the kingdom in preparation for the next chapter's discussion of the *basileia* vision of Jesus in utopian context.[3]

In general, it is safe to say that scholarship on the kingdom of God has been preoccupied with several key issues. First, the question of the correct translation of the phrase and its syntactical usage has received extensive discussion. Second, the tradition history of the phrase has been mined for insights into Jesus' usage. Third, the question of the temporal reference of the kingdom has been investigated: Is the kingdom of God a present or future reality? Fourth, the nature of the language of the kingdom has been interrogated: Is it a concept, a symbol, or a metaphor? Fifth, the kingdom has been interpreted politically, seeing Jesus as a revolutionary who aimed to establish divine rule by insurrection, through peaceful social reform, or through the proclamation of the imminent restoration of Israel. Finally, recent feminist scholarship has made a distinctive and insightful contribution to the discussion by speaking of the "kingdom of God movement" (or *basileia* movement) rather than the "Jesus movement" to describe the mission of Jesus and his earliest disciples, thus highlighting the importance of the message of the *basileia* rather than the identity of the proclaimer. On the following pages, each of these trajectories in the scholarship on the kingdom of God will be surveyed.

Matters of Translation and Syntax

The phrase *hē basileia tou theou* (or *tōn ouranōn*) has generally been related to the Hebrew expression *malkût shamayim* (Aramaic: *malkuta dishᵉmaya*; "kingdom of [the] heavens").[4] The Matthean variant *hē basileia tōn ouranōn* ("the kingdom of the heavens") is interpreted as a Jewish circumlocution for the divine name, otherwise synonymous with the more usual Gospel formula, *hē basileia tou theou*. Further, as Duling observes, it is typically argued that "the 'Kingdom of God/Heaven' is not primarily spatial, territorial, political, or national: therefore it should be translated as 'kingly rule,' 'reign,' or 'sovereignty' rather than 'kingdom.'"[5]

In a recent article, Roy A. Harrisville finds 149 references to the kingdom of God in the New Testament, most of them in Matthew (fifty-one references) and Luke (forty-nine references).[6] Mark has eighteen instances, and John only five, leaving twenty-six references in the other New Testament writings.[7] His analysis of the syntax of these references renders the following results.

In references in which the kingdom is construed as an object, in both the Gospels and other New Testament writings, "what 'happens' most to the kingdom of God is that it is 'entered.'"[8] The kingdom is also preached, inherited, sought or awaited, given or received, seized, shut up, promised, prepared, assigned, and shared.[9] Harrisville observes with respect to the most common verbs associated with the kingdom ("enter," "preach," "inherit") that they presuppose that "the kingdom somehow preexists, preceded, is prior to whatever fate it encounters.... The genitive in the phrase 'kingdom of God' is a subjective genitive—the kingdom belongs to God; God is its initiator and executor."[10] The kingdom is not brought into existence by the preaching of Jesus, nor is it something that belongs solely to the future, since it can be acted upon in the present by human beings.

There are few references to the kingdom as subject; in these, it either "comes" (*ephthasen*) or "approaches" (*eggiken*).[11] The parables are a more fertile source of *basileia* references. Of these, 70 percent are distinctively Matthean; the other instances are found "in the parable of the Sower (Mark 4:1-9), the Mustard Seed (Mark 4:30-32; Luke 13:18-19), the Leaven (Luke 13:20-21), and the Secretly Growing Seed (Mark 4:26-29)—the first three shared with Matthew (13:1-9, 31-32, 33) and the last peculiar to Mark."[12] Harrisville concludes that there is little textual basis for a spatial notion of the kingdom, since spatial references are confined to "a mere prepositional phrase" (e.g., "you are not far from the kingdom of God"; Mark 12:34)[13] or to a future promise of banqueting "in the kingdom."[14] He observes that the question of to whom the kingdom "belongs" can be answered mostly with reference to the beatitudes (to the poor [in spirit]; Matt 5:3; Luke 6:20; cf. James 2:5; to those persecuted for the sake of righteousness; Matt. 5:10) and to children (Matt 19:13-15; Mark 10:13-16; Luke 6:20). Some will be excluded from the kingdom (Matt 8:12; Luke 9:62), but others are "the children of the kingdom" (Matt 13:38).[15]

Of course, the references with the least claim to authenticity are the (relatively few) allusions to the kingdom of the Christ, or the Son of man, or of God and Christ. Mark contains no such references; Matthew and Luke together contain eight. Other New Testament usages include John 18:36, 1 Cor 15:24, Eph 5:5, and Col 1:13.[16] Significantly, such references never appear in parables, beatitudes, or blessings of children,[17] speech forms with a relatively high claim on authenticity.[18]

Tradition History

In an effort to understand the religious context of Jesus' preaching, scholars have studied the many and varied usages of the phrase "kingdom of God" (and similar formulas) in the Hebrew scriptures, especially the Psalms;[19] the Palestinian and Greek Pseudepigrapha; the Dead Sea Scrolls; works by hellenistic Jewish authors; ancient Jewish prayers; the rabbinic literature; and the New Testament and other early Christian writings.[20] In general, it can be observed that there is a development from the general notion that God is king over Israel and the world (Hebrew scriptures) to the apocalyptic idea that God's reign will be established eschatologically when God, with or without a messianic figure, judges the nations and rewards his people (Daniel, Palestinian Pseudepigrapha, DSS).[21] Aramaic synagogue prayers (Kaddish, *Shimoneh Esreh*) express the hope that God will soon establish his kingdom,[22] whereas the rabbinic literature tends to conceive of God's reign in individualistic, nonpolitical terms.[23] Jewish diaspora literature frequently expresses the notion that God is king (Tob 13:6, 7, 10, 11, 15; Jdt 9:12; Add Esth 13:15; 14:3b, 12; 2 Macc 1:24; 7:9; 13:4; 3 Macc 2:2; 6:2), sometimes with apocalyptic overtones (*Sib. Or.* 3–5).[24] The Stoic notion of the philosopher-sage as *basileus* governed by reason and virtue is appropriated by some hellenistic Jewish writers (4 Macc 2:23; 7:10; Wis 6:17-20; 10:9-10; Philo, *On the Life of Abraham* 26).[25]

Bruce Chilton helpfully summarizes the range of distinctive understandings of the kingdom in early Judaism (second century BCE to second century CE).[26] The Pharisaic understanding of kingdom conflated it with the observance of Torah; for them, Chilton asserts, to recite the *Shema* was to "take on the yoke of the kingdom" (Midrash *Berakoth* 2.2).[27] In the Aramaic Targums, "kingdom" tends to be used when the Hebrew text speaks of God's intervention on behalf of Israel (e.g., cf. Isa 40:9; Targum Isa 40:10).[28] In the Dead Sea Scrolls, the terms *king* and *kingdom* refer to God's celestial rule: "In the view of the Essenes [whom Chilton identifies as the community of the Scrolls], the community of the covenant joined themselves with the angels in worship, so that the reference of the kingdom certainly was not removed from how God might be known by his people" (e.g., *Songs of the Sabbath Sacrifice,* 4Q405 23.2.1–2).[29]

Hellenistic Jewish writings conceive of God's kingdom in terms of the providential ordering of creation through divine Wisdom (e.g., Wis 10:10): "When a righteous man fled from his brother's wrath, she [Wisdom] guided him on straight paths; she showed him *the kingdom of God,* and gave him knowledge of holy things; she prospered him in his labors, and increased the fruit of his toil."[30] Obviously, the several groups within early Judaism conceived of God's *basileia* differently. While the ancient Jewish understandings of the kingdom provide a necessary context for understanding Jesus' usage, it is unlikely that he simply adopted one or the other *tout court.*[31]

Future, Realized, or Inaugurated Eschatology?

Perhaps more than any other issue, the question of the temporal reference of the kingdom of God has occupied scholarship for the past hundred years or so. The three main options are a purely futuristic, apocalyptic kingdom; a realized eschatology, in which the kingdom is fully available in the present; or an "inaugurated" or partially realized eschatology, in which the kingdom is seen to have begun but to be fully manifested in the future. The scholarly discussion is lengthy and complex; the summary below attempts to capture the most influential positions.[32]

The first of these options, sometimes called "thoroughgoing" (or "consistent") eschatology, is especially associated with the germinal works of Johannes Weiss (1892) and Albert Schweitzer (1907).[33] Reacting against the argument of nineteenth-century liberal theology that the kingdom of God as preached by Jesus was a purely social and ethical concept, these German scholars interpreted Jesus as a fiery apocalyptic preacher who announced the imminent coming of the kingdom, synonymous with the end of the present cosmic order. When the end did not materialize, Jesus courted death in order to force his heavenly father to intervene.[34]

A consistently noneschatological interpretation of the kingdom is associated with C. H. Dodd's classic work on the parables of Jesus.[35] Dodd, against the consistent eschatologists, coined the term *realized eschatology* to typify Jesus' understanding of the kingdom of God. Jesus taught in parables, Dodd argued, as an assertion of his messianic identity: "Jesus' eschatology was 'realized' in the sense that he held that his hearers could personally and fully encounter God and God's promises in his own person."[36] For Dodd, the kingdom was present in the here-and-now in the quality of experience of the encounter between Jesus and his hearers.[37]

A third option that has been adopted by many scholars is the mediating position, often associated with the work of G. R. Beasley-Murray,[38] that while Jesus did view the kingdom of God as fully to be realized in the future, he also proclaimed its "inbreaking" into the present age. The "now-and-not-yet" explanation most satisfactorily comprehends both sayings about the future rule of God and the presence/fulfillment of the kingdom in the world of Jesus and his audience.[39]

Concept, Symbol, or Metaphor?

While the majority of scholars have treated the kingdom of God as a definable concept or idea, Norman Perrin distinguished between the kingdom as a univocal apocalyptic "sign" (apocalyptic usages) and Jesus' evocation of the kingdom as a multivalent "tensive symbol" that alludes to an ancient myth of God as king who had acted powerfully, and continued to act, in creation and in the history of Israel (see chapter 2 for full discussion).[40] Perrin found this myth invoked in a body of material in the Synoptics and the *Gospel of Thomas* that "competent scholarly opinion would recognize as authentic,"[41] including "kingdom sayings"; the Lord's Prayer; proverbial sayings; and the major parables. In such expressions, Jesus deliberately challenges the listener "to take the ancient myth with renewed seriousness, and to begin to anticipate the manifestation of the reality of which it speaks in the concrete actuality of their experience."[42] The petitions of the Lord's Prayer (which echoes the Kaddish prayer of the ancient synagogue) amount to "explorations of fundamental possibilities for the experience of God as king in human life."[43] The most radical of Jesus' proverbial kingdom sayings (e.g., eschatological reversal sayings like Mark 8:35; 10:23b, 25, 31; Luke 14:11), unlike traditional proverbs that convey conventional wisdom, function to jolt the listener into making a judgment upon existence in the world.[44] Thus, Jesus' kingdom language does not refer to a definable "concept" but mythopoeically portrays God's activity in the world in a way that demands an existential response from the hearer.[45]

Using the Targumic references to the kingdom of God (or "of the Lord"), Bruce Chilton has come to similar conclusions about the meaning of the phrase in Jesus' preaching: "The kingdom was not a régime, whether present or future at all. . . . Rather, Jesus was impelled to preach by his certainty that God would reveal himself powerfully; the kingdom announcement affirmed vividly but simply that God was acting and would act with strength on behalf of his people."[46] The Psalms are paradigmatic of this way of speaking about God's rule, which has five dimensions or coordinates:

1. Eschatological—the kingdom is portrayed as so near as to be present, but awaiting full disclosure (e.g., Psalms 44, 47, 96, 98).[47]

2. Transcendence—the kingdom is transcendent not in an abstract sense but in that it is universal, encompassing all of creation (e.g., Psalm 145).[48]

3. Judgment—God's kingdom demands justice and the punishment of the wicked; the human social order is incompatible with divine rule, but God's justice will inevitably triumph over evil (Psalms 9, 10, 97).[49]

4. Purity—Zion is God's holy mountain, and the sacrifices offered in God's temple must be pure (Psalms 24, 5, 103). Purity encompasses both ritual and ethical cleanness: "Those who are clean in that comprehensive sense are enabled to encounter God as he appropriates as his own what is offered purely."[50]

5. Radiance—in the Psalms, God's holiness is associated especially with the temple (Zion) and the heavens. The reign of God

radiates from Zion, as recognized first and foremost by the children of Israel, but also in heaven and ultimately by the whole earth (Psalms 47, 29, 114, 145).[51]

Chilton argues that Jesus' "map" of the kingdom of God shared these coordinates: "He had a view of God as king, a vision of the divine activity, that involved its eschatology, its transcendence, its ethics, its purity, and its radiance."[52] The eschatological dimension is expressed, for example, by the "your kingdom come" of the Lord's prayer.[53] The kingdom's transcendence is illustrated by the dynamic power expressed in sayings such as Matt 12:28//Luke 11:20 ("If I by the spirit cast out demons, then the kingdom of God has arrived among you") and the parable of the leaven (Matt 13:33//Luke 13:20-21//*Gosp. Thom.* 96).[54] The coordinate of judgment is expressed in the parable of the banquet (Matt 22:1-10//Luke 14:16-24//*Gosp. Thom.* 64) and sayings that refer to the relationship between the kingdom and wealth (Matt 19:23-24//Mark 10:23-25//Luke 18:24; Matt 13:44-46; *Gosp. Thom.* 76, 109).[55] The purity of the kingdom is evoked, for example, by Jesus' cleansing of a leper (Matt 8:2-4//Mark 1:40-44//Luke 5:12-14), his declaration of what is defiling (Matt 15:11//Mark 7:15), and his teachings on receiving the kingdom like a child (Mark 10:15//Luke 18:17).[56] The "pure kingdom" of Jesus will ultimately "radiate" into the whole earth, as the tiny mustard seed grows into a "tree" (Matt 13:31-32//Mark 4:30-32//Luke 13:18-19//*Gosp. Thom.* 20; see also Mark 11:17; Matt 11:12//Luke 16:16).[57] For Chilton, then, the kingdom is not a concept or event that can be fixed in time, space, or polity but a *theolegoumenon*—a complex and multifaceted metaphor expressing God's relationship to God's people and to the cosmos.[58]

Political Interpretations of the Kingdom[59]

The interpretations surveyed so far regard the kingdom primarily as a religious proclamation: they emphasize the theological/supernatural dimension of divine rule ("the kingdom *of God*"). However, an important minority of scholars have interpreted the kingdom in political terms, highlighting the *basileia* aspect of the phrase. One significant scholarly position arguing for a political interpretation is the "Jesus as revolutionary" hypothesis, most prominently associated with the work of S. G. F. Brandon.[60] According to Brandon, the evangelists' apologetic portrayal of a "pacific Christ," unjustly condemned by Jewish authorities, was contrived to obscure the reality that Jesus was a radical Jewish nationalist, executed under Pontius Pilate for sedition. Not only did Jesus publicly oppose the payment of taxes and lead an assault on the Temple, but he was also an advocate of armed resistance to Roman occupation. After his crucifixion Jesus' Judean followers continued his opposition to Rome, and the early Jewish-Christian church took part in the Jewish revolt of 66–70 CE. According to this hypothesis the "kingdom of God" proclaimed by Jesus involved the imminent overthrow of the Roman occupation by force.

As Marcus Borg notes, this interpretation has been deemed unsatisfactory by the majority of scholars.[61] A variant on this approach that has met with more scholarly acceptance is to interpret Jesus as a social (rather than political) radical who anticipated the establishment of God's reign through nonviolent social, economic, and religious means.[62] However, the effect of the emphasis on social, economic, and religious dimensions of the kingdom is to downplay any specifically *political* aspects of *hē basileia tou theou*. John Dominic Crossan, for example, sees Jesus in deliberate opposition to both Jewish religious partisanship and Roman authority, not through political protest but through "a combination of *free healing and common eating*, a religious and economic egalitarianism that negated alike and at once the hierarchical and patronal normalcies of Jewish religion and Roman power."[63] Jesus announced a "brokerless kingdom of God," where individuals were forced into "unmediated physical and spiritual contact with God and unmediated physical and spiritual contact with one another."[64] Despite his opposition to the Roman order, Crossan's "peasant Jewish Cynic" has little interest in the restoration of Jewish national independence.

A third approach that takes the politics of Jesus more seriously is represented by scholars such as G. B. Caird, G. R. Beasley-Murray, N. T. Wright, William R. Herzog, Richard A. Horsley and Scot McKnight.[65]

These scholars interpret Jesus as a religious/political reformer who spearheaded a movement to restore Israel to its ancient relationship with God, not through revolution but through covenant faithfulness. N. T. Wright sees the kingdom of God as a political slogan that captures the nationalistic hope, common to many ancient Jewish groups, that "Israel's god is going to rule Israel (and the whole world), and that Caesar, or Herod, or anyone else of their ilk, is not. It means that Torah will be fulfilled at last, that the Temple will be rebuilt and the Land cleansed. . . . It means that Israel's god will rule her in the way he intends, through properly appointed persons and means."[66] Richard Horsley and Neil Asher Silberman see Jesus as spearheading a grassroots peasant protest against the undermining of the social and economic fabric of village life by heavy taxation and the aristocratic appropriation of traditional landholdings:[67]

> In both Jesus' and John's preaching, the Kingdom of God meant a revolution in the way people behaved toward each other and their recognition that they should have no Caesars, tetrarchs, centurions, or other overlords above them except the one God and Creator of the world. In practical terms, that meant rejecting the rule of all powers and returning to the pure covenantal system under which Israelites—and indeed all peoples—would be considered to be brothers and sisters under God. In modern political terms, that might be called a revolution, but for Jesus and the people of his time, it was nothing more nor less than Israel's ancient legacy. And like earlier Israelite prophets whose public role he re-enacted, Jesus taught that Israel's non-kingly Kingdom could already be present and functioning in the land's fields, towns, and villages—if only people recognized its sanctity and reoriented their community life accordingly.[68]

Scot McKnight describes Jesus as an audacious preacher of the kingdom's arrival in and through his own agency: "Jesus firmly believed that he was the prophet of the last day whom God had appointed to usher in the kingdom."[69] The advent of the kingdom meant the restoration of the nation and the end of exile;[70] it was continuous with the covenants of Israel's sacred history, but Jesus also regarded his announcement of divine rule as "something new and restorative."[71] However, the kingdom also had a future dimension, when the new regime ushered in by Jesus would be consummated (although he was unsure as to when precisely it would arrive). Israel would be judged for its sinfulness, and Jerusalem would be destroyed; Israelites who survived the judgment and destruction would constitute the restored nation, which would be ruled by the new tribal leaders, the Twelve: "[He] believed that the final kingdom would be a time of endless fellowship with the Father, who would shower peace, love and justice on the land . . . the consummation of history, the goal toward which God had been directing his energies since the days of Abraham. It would be the complete end of exile and the restoration of God's people."[72] Although these scholars differ as to the particulars of the spiritual motivation and political strategy behind Jesus' proclamation of divine rule, there is general agreement that the *basileia* he envisioned was first and foremost a restored nation of Israel.

Feminist Contributions: Jesus within the Basileia Movement

In 1934, Rudolf Otto remarked that "it is not Jesus who brings the kingdom; on the contrary; the kingdom brings him with it. . . . His own activity lies in, and is carried forth by, the tidal wave of the divine victory."[73] Starting from a very different vantage point, some feminist biblical scholars have recently argued that Jesus was not the "founder" of a movement that centered on his personality or authority but *part* of a multifaceted Jewish quest for the reign of God in the Second Temple period.[74] As Jane D. Schaberg notes, this perspective construes the kingdom of God movement "as one of several renewal or revitalization groups within Judaism (such as the Therapeutae, John the Baptist's group, the Essenes of Qumran, Simon ben Giora's revolutionary movement)."[75] This understanding undercuts claims of the uniqueness of the so-called "Jesus movement" by considering it within the context of other Jewish movements with comparable themes and goals.

In response to Jewish feminist critiques of Christian feminist assertions that Jesus was unique among the Jews of his time in his treatment of women,[76] feminist historical-critical scholars have found evidence that the openness of Jesus' circle to women's participation was also a feature of some of the other diverse expressions of Second Temple Judaism.[77] That is, unlike "malestream" historical Jesus studies, feminist historical criticism has focused not on the heroic "great man" Jesus but on the community/movement to which he belonged (the "kingdom of God" or *basileia* movement) and which continued to develop after his death, one of several utopian/eutopian movements within first-century Judaism that was open to female membership and conceived, at least in part, in reaction against Roman imperial domination.[78] For example, in an article evocatively titled "Re-membering Jesus: Women, Prophecy, and Resistance in the Memory of the Early Churches," Mary Rose D'Angelo locates "Jesus the prophet within a prophetic movement" that included other men and women prophets of Sophia/spirit seeking "a movement out of Caesar's reign, a literal moving out from under the imperial order."[79] Following D'Angelo, Elisabeth Schüssler Fiorenza speaks of the "emancipatory *basileia*-movement" in which Jesus participated.[80] For Schaberg, Jesus is one of many "leaders" of this movement, along with other disciples, both male and female.[81] While this approach has some affinities with the "restorationist" interpretations discussed above, it differs significantly by relativizing both Jesus (within the *basileia* movement) and the movement itself (among other Jewish renewal movements).

A Glimpse of the Kingdom

Despite the vast amounts of interpretation that the phrase has inspired, it is difficult, from reading most of the scholarship, to describe or visualize what the kingdom of God would be like, once established. On the purely futuristic interpretation, this is understandable, since, in general, apocalyptic discourse is more preoccupied with detailing events that will precede the establishment of God's reign than with describing what it will be like. Interpretations that see the kingdom as already present in the ministry of Jesus—whether in the form of the "realized eschatology" of C. H. Dodd or the liberal theological formulations of the nineteenth century—have often described an "ethical" or "spiritual" realm that is, as Duling notes, atemporal.[82] Harrisville's observation that the kingdom of God *preexists* Jesus is a useful addition to the discussion of the temporal reference of the term; it complements the position of (especially) Perrin and Chilton that Jesus' usage was a development of traditional Jewish mythic/theological language expressing the presence and power of God in the world, as well as the feminist argument that the movement to which Jesus belonged was one among several Jewish groups "seeking the kingdom of God" (cf. Mark 15:43).

Recent studies that place the *basileia* movement within the context of Jewish nationalism in the Second Temple period are a useful historical corrective to the overemphasis in some classic interpretations on individual response to the message of Jesus (e.g., in different ways, Schweitzer, Dodd, Perrin). Arguments that Jesus conceived of the kingdom as present or "inaugurated" in his ministry render a glimpse of the contours of the divine realm; if his own prophetic activity was the sign or substance of its dawning, then Jesus' fondness for banqueting, his exorcisms and healings, and his proclamation of hope to the poor, hungry, and sorrowful reveal the shape of the kingdom.[83]

JESUS' PREACHING *of the* KINGDOM *of* GOD *in* UTOPIAN CONTEXT

5

As the last chapter has shown, the analysis of the phrase *hē basileia tou theou* as a key theme in Jesus' preaching has generated a large volume of scholarship over the last century. Surprisingly, in view of the long tradition of biblical utopian thinking, the utopian character of Jesus' proclamation of the kingdom of God has not been brought into the discussion. This chapter will offer a fresh perspective on the significance of the kingdom in the teaching and preaching of Jesus by interpreting it in the context of Graeco-Roman, biblical, and hellenistic Jewish utopian thinking, with particular reference to descriptions of ideal societies (utopianism) and ideas about divine rule (theocracy). In addition, the work of Doron Mendels on Jewish nationalism in ancient Palestine will be used to assess the historical Jesus' attitude to native rule.[1]

Utopianism

Utopian thinking has a history that goes back thousands of years, and it was very much a part of hellenistic/Graeco-Roman political theorizing and literary expression. Scholars of utopian studies have sometimes classified Judaeo-Christian conceptions of the kingdom of God as among the many utopian traditions of antiquity.[2] However, since most utopian scholars have limited knowledge of biblical scholarship, they tend to portray the kingdom of God as a universally understood and undifferentiated expression of a uniquely Jewish "messianism," without sufficient awareness of the range of meanings of the phrase within Judaism or of possible connections with other hellenistic/Graeco-Roman conceptions of ideal societies.

In fact, as argued in chapter 2, the tendency of the Jewish scriptural tradition generally is to portray the history of Israel in utopian terms: as the divinely promised "land flowing with milk and honey," as the powerful tribal federation established under the leadership of Joshua, as the golden age of David and Solomon, or as the ethnically uniform hierocracy of Ezra-Nehemiah. This utopian propensity is carried through in the varied prophetic expressions of hope for a future ideal age. In hellenistic/Graeco-Roman times, Jewish utopianism is often expressed in apocalyptic terms, although other expressions are possible. For example, Jesus Sirach's discourse (Sir 44:1-50) in praise of "famous men" (v. 20) is a litany of utopian moments in Israel's history, culminating in the glorious reign in Jerusalem of the high priest Simon son of Onias (219–196 BCE), the sage's near contemporary. The antimessianic author of Pseudo-Philo's *Biblical Antiquities* (c. 70 CE) presents the charismatic leadership of the judges as a foil for the Israelite monarchy.[3]

In most cases, early Jewish hopes for a *future* utopian age hark back to idealized eras in the sacred history, interpreted as models of divinely sanctioned rule to be implemented perfectly in the future. As Jonathan Z. Smith observes, Jewish hopes for the future are typically *locative*, envisioning the land of Israel or Jerusalem and its environs, rather than some remote isle of the blessed, as the ultimate "good place."[4] The most frequently evoked template for the future is the united monarchy of David and (especially) Solomon, when "Judah and Israel dwelt safely, every man under his vine and under his fig tree, from Dan to Beer-Sheba, all the days of Solomon" (1 Kgs 5:5; cf. Mic 4:4). However, the future idyll can be portrayed as a return to Eden; as an eschatological state of Jubilee (Luke 4:16-21; 11QMelch 2:1-9; *Jub.* 23:26-31); as the restoration of the land promised to the children of Israel in the time of Moses (Jer 31; 32:40-41; Mal 3:17–4:6); or in terms of return from exile (e.g., Dan 9:2). The prophetic tradition eulogizes even the period of Israel's wilderness wanderings as a time of covenant faithfulness (Jer 2:2; 31:2; Ezek 34:25; Hos 2:14; 9:10; 13:5-6; Amos 2:10; cf. Neh 9:21). In early Judaism both the Essenes and the Zealots seem to have imagined themselves as "wilderness" communities, as did the Therapeutai/Therapeutrides—perhaps in anticipation of the imminent restoration of the Promised Land (cf. *War* 2.258–63; Philo, *Contemplative Life* 2).[5] Philo does not harbor any hopes for a renewal of Jewish sovereignty, but idealizes the "kingship" of certain figures in Israel's remote past: Adam, Melchizedek, Abraham, and especially Moses (*Life of Moses* 1.148–54).

Arguably the oldest reported utopian communities are Jewish: the Essenes in Judea and the Therapeutai/Therapeutrides in Egypt (see chapter 3). According to Mendels, not only did the Essenes regard themselves as the "New Israel," but they were founded under the direct influence of hellenistic utopian literature, especially Iambulus's fictional Islands of the Sun.[6] As we have seen, a good case can also be made that the Therapeutai/Therapeutrides were similarly influenced by the hellenistic utopian romantic tradition, as well as by scriptural ideals.

Divine Rule (Theocracy)

The philosopher R. S. Bluck defines theocracy as follows:

> A theocracy, we may say, is a state wherein the sanction of
> all law lies not in any man-made code, or even in the will

or opinions of one or more human rulers, but in absolute standards revealed to man by divine agency, so that in
theory at least the real ruler of the community is the divine
agency that sets the standards, while the earthly "rulers" are
in the nature of High Priests whose task is to interpret and
enforce them. The exact nature of the divine agency concerned is irrelevant to the definition; what matters is that
the ultimate author of all law, whether written or unwritten, be said to be divine. Such was the case, of course, with
the Jewish community at the time of Moses.[7]

The idea that divine rule was exercised through the medium of human
kingship (*basileia*) was a commonplace of Graeco-Roman political
thought, for the king was considered to be the godlike representative
and revealer of the divine law of nature in his realm. The hellenistic
ideal of kingship is well expressed by the Pythagorean Diotogenes in
the first century CE:

> For the Best must be honored by the best man, and the
> Governing Principle by one who is a governor. So just as
> God is the Best of those things which are most honor-
> able by nature, likewise the king is best in the earthly and
> human realm. Now the king bears the same relation to the
> state [*polin*] as God to the world; and the state is in the
> same ratio to the world as the king is to God. For the state,
> made as it is by a harmonizing together of many different
> elements, is an imitation of the order and harmony of the
> world, while the king who has an absolute rulership, and
> is himself Animate Law, has been metamorphosed into a
> deity among men.[8]

Of course, the ideology of divine kingship has deep roots in the
ancient Middle East and finds Israelite expression in the tradition
that the Davidic king is the adopted son of YHWH (1 Sam 7:14; Ps
2:7). Philo develops this tradition by interpreting the "kingdom of
God" (*basileia tou theou*) as the imprint of the divine Torah on the

soul of the wise king; thus the human king/sage reflects the image of the divine archetype (*On the Special Laws* 4.164; cf. Wis 6:17-21; 10:10). Philo could also use the term *basileia* to refer to the mind's or wisdom's control over the sage and his affairs (*basileia tou sophou*) or to God's control over the mind of the wise man (Philo, *On Abraham* 261; *On the Change of Names* 135; *Life of Moses* 2.241; *On the Special Laws* 1.207). As Burton Mack observes, this hellenistic Jewish language of the kingdom emanates from wisdom circles, not apocalyptic tradition, which (according to Mack) never explicitly uses the "kingdom of God/heaven" formula.[9] However, it could also emanate from the Deuteronomistic history and the covenantal hope associated with it (cf. Deut 17:14-20; 1 Kgs 5:5-15; see also Exod 19:6).

Surprisingly, the term *theocracy* was not coined by an ancient political philosopher or by a contemporary social scientist, but by a first-century Palestinian Jew. In the course of explaining the unique polity of the Jewish people for Gentile readers, Josephus coins a new word, "theocracy" (*theokratia*):

> There is endless variety in the details of the customs and laws which prevail in the world at large. To give but a summary enumeration: some peoples have entrusted the supreme political power to monarchies, others to oligarchies, yet others to the masses. Our lawgiver, however, was attracted by none of these forms of polity, but gave to his constitution the form of what—if a forced expression be permitted—may be termed a "theocracy" [*theokratia apedeiche to politeuma*], placing all sovereignty and authority in the hands of God.[10]

The law governs the Jewish people dispersed throughout the world, who voluntarily follow its precepts no matter where they may be (2.220). Josephus suggests that if the Jewish nation and its laws were not known to exist by "all the world," they are so exalted that a Greek audience would regard an account of them as a figment of the imagination of the lecturer (2.221). Josephus may be implicitly contrasting the Jewish nation with fictional utopias like Panchaïa, Hyperborea, the

Islands of the Sun, or even Atlantis; he explicitly refers to Plato, whom, though widely admired, is often scoffed at by "expert statesmen" for the "futile, brilliant but very fanciful" nature of his dialogues (2.224–25). Although the Jews of Josephus's time were stateless, they continued to obey their ancestral laws, an ideal polity that neither Greek romancers nor philosophers were able to imagine.

For Josephus, writing in the last decades of the first century, the best mediator of theocratic rule in the sacred past had been "aristocratic" rule by a council of elders (*gerousia*) as practiced in the time before Saul (*Jewish Antiquities* 4.223–24; 5.135),[11] as opposed to the corrupt, unqualified, and foolish priests who had held that position in the decades preceding the Jewish rebellion (see *Jewish Antiquities* 15.22; 20.180–81, 199–203, 213–14, 216–18, 224–51).[12] The destruction of the Temple by the Romans had been divinely mandated (*War* 5.288–315), and kingship over the Jews had been handed on by God to Vespasian, the Roman emperor acclaimed in Judea (*War* 6.312–13; cf. 3.399–408; 4.585–629).[13]

Although like other Jews of his time, Josephus looks back to a (in Josephus's case, premonarchic) "golden age" of divine rule over Israel, in his late work, *Against Apion* (c. 95–100 CE), the historian portrays his Jewish contemporaries in highly idealized terms as an *international* community regulated by the Mosaic law. The Jews dispersed throughout the world, claims Josephus, are a people whose law teaches them to love and not to hate each other; to share with one another; to oppose injustice and practice righteousness; to be hardworking, frugal, and content with their labors; to make war not for gain, but only to defend the law; to punish evildoers; to avoid sophistry; and to let their actions speak for themselves (2.291–93):

> I would therefore boldly maintain that we have introduced
> to the rest of the world a very large number of very beauti-
> ful ideas. What greater beauty than inviolable piety? What
> higher justice than obedience to the laws? What more ben-
> eficial than to be in harmony with one another, to be a
> prey neither to disunion in adversity nor to arrogance and
> faction in prosperity; in war to despise death, in peace to
> devote oneself to crafts or agriculture; and to be convinced

> that everything in the whole universe is under the eye and
> the direction of God?

For Josephus, theocratic rule, whether humanly mediated by Moses himself, by the elders of Israel, or by the Jewish nation dispersed throughout the Roman Empire, was the unique contribution of the Jewish people to the world, admired by others and epitomized by the Jews of the diaspora. Josephus's invention of the term *theocracy* may be interpreted as a Jewish response to a concrete political reality that Josephus knew all too well: the recent Jewish attempt to restore native rule to the homeland had failed, and the Jewish nation-state was truly defunct. If God's rule over the Jewish people was going to endure, it would have to be without a Jewish ruler, Temple, or nation-state.

Y. Amir has argued that Josephus's idea of *theokratia* is not related to the kingdom of heaven/God as it was conceived in the Second Temple period: "In the Hebrew of that time the term מלך '*melekh*' always appears in the phrase '*melekh al kol ha-aretz*' מלך על כל האוץ (king over the whole world) and never in the context . . . מלך ישראל '*melekh Yisrael*' (king of Israel). In the religious thought of Josephus' time, the phrase 'Kingdom of Heaven' denotes a cosmic entity, to which even the Angels are considered subordinate."[14] However, Amir fails to note that Josephus actually uses *theokratia* in an earthly sense, in that God's rule is exercised over the Jewish people dispersed *throughout the world*; indeed, for Josephus, Jews simply recognize the fact of God's universal rule *more perfectly* than non-Jews. Further, Amir's assertion that in the Second Temple period the idea of the universal rule of God had replaced more particularistic notions of divine kingship is simply not borne out by the evidence (e.g., 2 Chron 13:8; 28:5; Dan 2:44; 7:27; Obad 1:21; *Jub.* 1:28; *1 En.* 90:20; *T. Mos.* 10; *T. Dan* 5:13; *Pss. Sol.* 17).[15]

The idea that the legitimate leadership of Israel is imparted by divine authority is so ubiquitous in the biblical and postbiblical tradition that it is difficult to conceive of a hellenistic Jew denying that the kingship of Israel, however it might be practically implemented, ultimately belonged to God.[16] Josephus's distinctive conception of the Jewish polity as a theocracy, either at home or in diaspora, epitomizes an ancient Israelite precept: "Indeed, all the earth is mine, but you shall be to me a priestly kingdom and a holy nation" (Exod 19:6; cf. Deut 7:6; 14:2; 26:18). As Talmon notes, taken as a whole, the Jewish biblical tradition represents universalism ("all the earth is mine") and particularity ("you shall be to me a priestly kingdom") not as opposites but as complementary: "the universalistic orientation, which in the Hebrew Bible appears especially, but not exclusively, in prophetic literature, is in no way impaired by the recognition of Israel's particularity, to which both the prophets and other biblical thinkers equally subscribe: Israel is God's chosen people in the community of nations."[17]

In virtually all of the "utopian eras" remembered by the biblical and extrabiblical Jewish authors, and in the prophetic and apocalyptic hopes for an ideal future Israel, God's rule is the source and authorization for legitimate political leadership, whether it be prophetic, charismatic, priestly, kingly, gerontocratic, or messianic. While Josephus agreed that the human right to rule over Israel was divinely ordained, God's mandate to rule both Israel and the known world had now been granted to a Roman, Vespasian. Under this legitimate human authority, God still reigned over the Jews (through the medium of Torah) and over the universe. Josephus's particular interpretation of *theokratia* approaches an early expression of the principle of the separation of religion and state; the polity of the Jews dispersed throughout the world, governed by their "sacred laws," is purely religious, exercised through the nonpolitical medium of the *prostasia* ("collegium") led by priests.[18] The historian's description of Jewish theocracy as an "invisible kingdom" dispersed throughout the world is also somewhat reminiscent of the present-oriented *basileia* sayings attributed to Jesus:

> "You won't be able to observe the coming of the kingdom of God. People are not going to be able to say, 'Look, here it is!' or 'Over there!' On the contrary, the kingdom of God is right here in your presence." (Luke 17:20b-21)

> "It will not come by watching for it. It will not be said, 'Look, here!' Or 'Look, there!' Rather, the father's kingdom is spread out upon the earth, and people don't see it." (*Gos. Thom.* 113)

"The kingdom of Heaven is like leaven which a woman took and concealed in fifty pounds of flour until it was all leavened." (Matt 13:33//Luke 13:20-21//*Gos. Thom.* 96)

"To what should we compare the kingdom of God, or what parable should we use for it? Consider the mustard seed: When it is sown on the ground, though it is the smallest of all the seeds on the earth; yet when it is sown, it comes up, and becomes the biggest of all garden plants, and produces branches, so that the birds of the sky can nest it its shade." (Mark 4:30-32//Matt 13:31-32//Luke 13:18-19// *Gos. Thom.* 20)

"The kingdom of Heaven is like treasure hidden in a field: when someone finds it, that person covers it up again, and out of sheer joy goes and sells every last possession and buys that field. Again, the kingdom of heaven is like some trader looking for beautiful pearls. When that merchant finds one priceless pearl, he sells everything he owns and buys it." (Matt 13:44-45//*Gos. Thom.* 109; 76)

"The kingdom of God is like this: Suppose someone sows seed on the ground, and sleeps and rises night and day, and the seed sprouts and matures, although the sower is unaware of it. The earth produces fruit on its own, first a shoot, then a head, then mature grain on the head." (Mark 4:26b-27)

"The kingdom is like a woman who was carrying a [jar] full of meal. While she was walking along [a] distant road, the handle of the jar broke and the meal spilled behind her [along] the road. She didn't know it; she hadn't noticed a problem. When she reached her house, she put the jar down and discovered it was empty." (*Gos. Thom.* 97)[19]

Such sayings about the presence of God's *basileia* in the world can also be compared with the Pharisaic *havurah*, which took on the discipline of divine rule through strict Torah observance while functioning within the larger Jewish society.

Jesus in Political Context

Doron Mendels, who considers the career of Jesus within the context of Jewish nationalism prior to 70 CE, remarks on the "non-political" tenor of his preaching of the kingdom.[20] In fact, with very few exceptions (e.g., Luke 22:30; cf. Matt 19:28), the *basileia* sayings attributed to Jesus by the evangelists—whether they express a present, futurist, or inaugurated eschatology—are remarkably free of nationalistic content: they do not associate the kingdom of God with "Israel" as a hoped-for national, political entity.[21] The few sayings that seem to equate kingship with Israel's rulers predict its demise (Matt 21:43; Luke 13:28-29//Matt 8:11-12) or are critical of it (Luke 6:16//Matt 11:12; Mark 12:35-38//Matt 22:41-46//Luke 20:41-44).[22] Unlike many Second Temple Jews, Jesus does not hark back to any of the utopian eras in the history of Israel as a template for the *basileia*. This is not to say that the announcement of the kingdom was not conceived by Jesus as continuous with and in fulfillment of the sacred history of Israel. Nor does it mean that Jesus denied the sanctity of the Temple[23] or of the land. However, the evidence suggests that Jesus' interpretation of the kingdom stressed the comprehensiveness of divine rule rather than its particularity. Even more than Josephus, Jesus seems to have emptied what Oscar Cullmann called the "Jewish theocratic solution" of concrete political overtones.[24] Mendels interprets this as implying that, for Jesus, the *basileia tou theou* was a transcendental kingdom, to be ruled by him as a purely spiritual messiah: "He wanted to be some kind of spiritual king, not a physical or political one. . . . He wanted it to remain as vague as possible."[25] Mendels contrasts the nebulousness of Jesus' *basileia* with "concrete plans" devised by the hellenistic utopists[26] and the Davidic-messianic hopes of some of his contemporaries.[27] It can also be contrasted with the tendency of the early Jewish utopists to conceptualize the kingdom of God in terms of the nation of Israel in some idealized historical era.

Mendels situates Jesus historically in the context of Jewish attitudes to *basileia* from the Roman occupation (63 BCE) to the end of the Bar Kochba Revolt (135 CE),[28] a period marked by "the accelerating decline of Jewish kingship."[29] In Jesus' time, the idea that an actual "king of the Jews" was a viable option had been undermined by the civil strife that marked the end of the Hasmonean dynasty, by the Roman occupation, and by the disreputable reign of the hellenizer Herod, who damaged his slender claim to legitimate rule by murdering the last of the Hasmoneans.[30] Even in Herod's time, Mendels observes, there were "a great many Jews who preferred peace, even under Roman aegis, to any sort of political unrest";[31] after Herod's death, a delegation to Rome supported by more than eight thousand Roman Jews wanted to abolish the kingship and create a Roman-ruled state. "In fact, many groups in the Diaspora were unhappy with Jewish kingship altogether, and even felt embarrassed at certain junctures by the Jewish state."[32] The 4 BCE riot in Jerusalem over the succession to the throne, crushed by the Romans in that year, added to the skepticism regarding native kingship.[33] Jesus lived in a partitioned Palestine, where a certain amount of local patriotism had supplanted Jewish nationalism, although Jerusalem maintained its religious and spiritual significance.[34] After the death of Agrippa I (44 CE), the last *basileus* of Judaea, the idea that native Jewish sovereignty was a live issue seems to have fallen into abeyance until the disastrous revolt of 66–70 CE.[35]

Jesus, then, lived during the low point in a decline of popular regard for Jewish kingship as a desirable political reality or source of spiritual leadership. The lack of concrete political content in Jesus' *basileia* sayings—the stress on the universality of God's rule, the absence of allusions to any of the "ideal" periods in Israel's past as templates for the kingdom, the vagueness of its temporal referents—bespeaks not a political or "restorationist" Jesus, or even (contra Mendels) an apolitical Jesus, who wanted to be the messiah of a spiritual kingdom. Rather, it suggests an anti-political Jesus, who used the phrase in a manner that deliberately downplayed explicitly nationalistic, restorationist, and particularistic overtones and aspirations,[36] although, to be sure, to be "antipolitical" is to take a political stand much as to be an atheist is to make a theological statement. In postcolonial terms Jesus' paradoxical conception of a nonpolitical "kingdom of God" could be described as his attempt to grapple with (or elide) Israel's complex history as both colonizer and colonized; as Leela Gandhi observes, "the postcolonial dream of discontinuity is ultimately vulnerable to the infectious residue of its own unconsidered and unresolved past."[37]

If, as some interpreters assert, Jesus used the language of the kingdom to subvert Roman imperialism,[38] he may have wished to disavow *Jewish* dreams of *basileia* as well. Needless to say, Mendels's assumption that Jesus regarded *himself* as a kingly or messianic figure, spiritual or otherwise, does not fit the evidence; no *basileia* saying of Jesus that has any claim on authenticity implies that Jesus regarded anyone but God as the legitimate king of Israel. The few references to Jesus as "king of Israel" are either ironic, placed on the lips of his adversaries (Mark 15:32; Matt 27:42), or expressions of Johannine Christology (John 1:49; 6:15; 12:13-15). Likewise, when the phrase "son of David" is applied to Jesus, the evangelists placed it on the lips of others (Matt 12:23; 15:22; 20:30-31; 21:9, 15; Mark 10:47-48; Luke 18:38-39); elsewhere, Jesus even questions the Messiah's Davidic lineage (Mark 12:35-37; Matt 22:42-45; Luke 20:41-44).[39] Jesus' reference to "his" kingdom in Luke 22:29-30 is otherwise unattested.[40] The famous saying about giving to Caesar what is Caesar's (Mark 12:17; Matt 22:21; Luke 20:25; *Gosp. Thom.* 100) wittily skirts the question of whether or not to pay the Roman poll tax, but it tacitly allows payment—a policy later commended by Paul (cf. Rom 13:6-7).[41]

One element in Jesus' praxis that seems to negate the argument for a non-nationalist Jesus is his calling of the Twelve (Mark 3:13-19; Matt 10:1-4; Luke 6:12-16). The symbolism behind Jesus' selection of a core group of twelve disciples seems obvious: "Twelve symbolizes the twelve tribes of Israel, which represent the descendants of Jacob. The twelve disciples of Jesus would thus have symbolized the new 'Israel' being created by Jesus."[42] If the Twelve were a feature of Jesus' career, the conclusion that the restoration of Israel to its ancient territorial sovereignty seems inevitable. As Scot McKnight asserts:

> In Jesus' world, the arrival of the kingdom involved a cluster of events: the end of the exile, the defeat of Rome, the return of the scattered tribes to the promised land, the restoration of pure worship in the temple, and the coming of God in full glory to Zion. . . .
>
> To his special followers, Jesus says:
>
>> "You are those who have stood by me in my trials; and I confer on you, just as my Father has conferred on me, a kingdom, so that you may eat and drink at my table in my kingdom, and you will sit on thrones judging the twelve tribes of Israel." (Luke 22:28-30//Matt. 19:28)
>
> That is, those who respond to Jesus now are those who will share the benefits of the kingdom that Jesus is presently inaugurating for Israel.[43]

However, the evidence for the historicity of the Twelve is equivocal. On the one hand, the tradition does pass the criteria of multiple attestation (Mark 3:13-19; Luke 22:30//Matt 19:28; 1 Cor 15:5) and of "embarrassment," since members of the Twelve are often portrayed negatively:

> The identification of Judas as one of the twelve (Mark 14:10, John 6:17), if historical, must have been an embarrassment to the early community. Other members of this circle are portrayed unfavorably: Peter deserts Jesus at his arrest; Thomas doubts; James and John, sons of Zebedee, the Thunder brothers, want special positions in the coming kingdom. At other times, the twelve argue about which of them is greatest and are represented as dense and without understanding.[44]

On the other hand, as Funk and his coauthors observe, there are many reasons to be skeptical about the Twelve: they are not mentioned in the earliest stratum of Q or in the *Gospel of Thomas*; the designation appears in the title of the *Didache* but not in the text; the letters of Clement and Ignatius do not mention them. Paul mentions the Twelve (1 Cor 15:5) but does not seem to recognize them as a special group of leaders, although he does speak of the three "pillars" (Cephas, James, and John) in Jerusalem (Gal 2:1-10).[45] Perhaps most damagingly to the historicity of the Twelve, they are never mentioned in the sayings of Jesus.

In view of these arguments, there is good reason to doubt that Jesus designated an inner circle of twelve disciples. However, even if *hoi dōdeka* were a feature of Jesus' ministry, this does not necessarily mean that Jesus anticipated the literal restoration of the tribes of Israel under the leadership of the Twelve. There is no reference to the tribal affiliations of these disciples, and no saying refers to an eschatological leadership role for them, apart from a single Q saying (Luke 22:30// Matt 19:28), which speaks of the disciples judging the twelve tribes of Israel.[46] Because the theme of the kingdom of God is so prominent in Jesus' sayings, the appointment of the Twelve could symbolize the premonarchic theocratic constitution of Israel, when the tribes were ruled by God alone rather than by a human king (cf. the harsh divine and prophetic indictment of the imposition of human kingship over Israel in 1 Sam 8:4-18).

Kingdom and Utopia

Jesus, then, did not subscribe to the kind of nationalistic, restorationist theology attributed to him by some scholars. This does not mean that the historical Jesus would not, under ideal circumstances, have welcomed a return to native rule over the traditional territory of Israel, that he was not in favor of the Jews of the diaspora returning to their homeland, or that he did not subscribe to the ancient doctrine that Israel was God's chosen people. However, for Jesus, the kingdom of God was not a hoped-for restoration of political independence to the Jewish nation but an evocation of the myth of God as king. As such, the kingdom was preexistent, since God had ruled the world since its creation; it was a present reality, since God's kingship was eternal; it would be manifested perfectly in the future, as the prophets had foretold. God's rule was exercised over the entire earth, but especially over Israel, God's chosen people.

As Josephus's account of *theokratia* illustrates, divine rule did not have to be exercised through a Jewish prophet, priest, or king; even a Roman emperor could be designated by God to rule Israel, in the homeland or in diaspora (cf. Isa 44:28). Jesus' emphasis on the universal aspect of the rule of God fits well within the range of Jewish political sentiments in his lifetime, which, as Mendels has shown, were inclined to be suspicious of native Jewish aspirations to kingship. The lack of any consistent portrayal of the kingdom in terms of some idealized age in Israel's past complements the cosmic interpretation of God's rule and suggests that Jesus' utopianism emphasized the "no-place" (*ou-topos*)—or perhaps even better, "everyplace" or "pantopian"— character of the kingdom. For Jesus, although God is the rightful and only true king of Israel and of the earth, the kingdom is *not* simply Israel, past, present, or future,[47] but, similarly to Josephus's portrayal of the Jewish polity in *Against Apion*, it is everywhere and nowhere, not "here" or "there" but present to those who recognize it (Luke 17:21; *Gos. Thom.* 3; 113).

If the conduct of those in the *basileia* movement can be taken as indicating how life under divine rule ought to be lived, then the teachings of Jesus regarding the "constitution" of *hē basileia tou theou* suggest an outline of the contours of the kingdom. If, as many scholars argue, Jesus' message was in continuity with John the Baptist's, then the kingdom of God was characterized by repentance and the pursuit of righteousness (Matt 3:2; Mark 1:4; Luke 3:3; Josephus, *Jewish Antiquities* 5.2).[48] Children and childlike behavior were paradigmatic of the kingdom (Matt 19:14//Mark 10:14-15//Luke 18:16; Matt 18:3; cf. *Gosp. Thom.* 22);[49] wealth was an impediment to "entering" it (Matt 19:24//Mark 10:25//Luke 18:25). The patriarchal family was rejected in favor of the community of disciples (Matt 8:22; 22:48-50; Mark 3:33-35; Luke 8:21; 9:59-60; 14:26; *Gosp. Thom.* 55; 99; 101), with God as their "father" (Matt 6:9; Luke 11:2b; cf. Matt 23:9). And more than twenty years of feminist biblical scholarship have made it clear that women were an important part of the *basileia* movement.[50]

The *basileia* movement of Jesus' time, like other Jewish utopian sects, was Torah-observant. As Jewish biblical scholar Paula Fredriksen notes, Jesus' attitude to the law of Moses, as illustrated by his ethical teachings, is both more lenient and more stringent than the attitudes of some of his contemporaries:

> Jesus . . . if we can judge by some synoptic passages and from the Q material surviving in the Sermon on the Mount, extended and intensified the Torah's commands. But—as we should expect from the lay leader of a lay movement— he focused on those given to all Israel, the Ten Command- ments, and he concentrated on the moral aspects of these. Thus Torah condemns murder; Jesus, even anger (Ex 20:13; Dt 5:17; Mt 5:22). Torah condemns adultery; Jesus, even the feeling of lust (Ex 20:14; Dt 5:18 Mt 5:28). Torah con- demns swearing falsely, taking God's name in vain; Jesus swearing itself (Ex 20:7; Lv 19:12; Mt 5:34). And when a scribe asks, "Which commandment is the first of all?" Jesus answers by referring to those commands directed to the entire people: Deuteronomy (the first line of the *sh'ma*) and Leviticus: "The first is, 'Hear O Israel, the Lord our God is One. And you shall love the Lord your God with all your heart, and with all your soul, and with all your strength.' And the second is this, 'Love your neighbor as yourself.' There is no other commandment greater than these" (Mk 12:28-31 and parr.).[51]

Fredriksen observes that Jesus' teaching in the Sermon on the Mount is not against Torah; rather, it intensifies Torah: "Jesus here does what the later rabbis will term 'building a fence around the Torah'; that is, he prescribes rules of behavior that extend the prohi- bition, thus ensuring that the biblical command cannot be broken."[52]

Jesus' pronouncement that it is not what goes into a person but what goes out of a person that defiles (Matt 15:10-11; Mark 7:14-15; *Gosp. Thom.* 14) is, Fredriksen holds, "reasonably uncontroversial."[53] Jesus is simply overstating his case in order to make a point, not repudiating Jewish dietary laws altogether (as the Marcan redaction insists [Mark 7:19b]).[54]

Contrary to Mendels's assertion that the kingdom proclaimed by Jesus was "vague" by comparison with those of hellenistic utopian writers,[55] the *basileia*, grounded as it is in the Hebrew scriptures, nonetheless shares many characteristics with the hellenistic utopias discussed in chapter 2 and with the accounts of the Essenes and Therapeutai/Therapeutrides in Philo and Josephus. Of course, as with the Essenes and Therapeutai, it is difficult to gauge the extent to which the sayings tradition has been given a utopian cast by the hellenized authors who describe it. Luke-Acts portrays the earliest church in utopian terms (cf. especially Acts 4:32-37), and Matthew depicts Jesus as the second Moses (Matt 5:1—7:28); obviously, the Gospel writers could, like Philo and Josephus with the Essenes and Therapeutai, paint the ministry of Jesus in terms influenced by scriptural and hellenistic utopias. However, unlike the Therapeutai and possibly the Essenes, we do have a body of sayings that have been mined by the Jesus Seminar and others for authentic Jesus material. Further, if Jesus is conceived as *part* of a larger *basileia* movement (perhaps initiated by the preaching of John the Baptist and extending past Jesus' lifetime), then a broader range of sayings can be admitted as indicative of their ethos at an early stage.

First and most obvious, the very notion of *hē basileia tou theou* is utopian in and of itself. As noted earlier, Josephus, coining the similar term *theokratia*, admits that this distinctively Jewish system of governance is so sublime that Greeks would mistake it for a romantic fantasy. In the famous "reversal" sayings, beatitudes, and similar traditions, the kingdom has a Saturnalian quality: the first will be last and the last first (Matt 19:30//Mark 10:31; 20:16//Luke 13:30//*Gosp. Thom.* 4; cf. Matt 20:1-15); leaders must be slaves to all (Matt 23:11; Mark 9:35; 10:44);[56] the poor, hungry, and dejected are blessed (Matt

5:3//Luke 6:20; *Gosp. Thom.* 54; Matt 5:6//Luke 6:21a//*Gosp. Thom.* 69; Matt 5:4//Luke 6:21b); enemies are loved (Matt 5:44b; Luke 6:27b, 32, 35a).[57]

Several of the most significant of the utopian themes shared by the Therapeutai, the Essenes, and the Heliopolitans discussed in chapter 4 can also be detected in the words of Jesus about the *basileia*. As discussed above, the rejection of biological family ties in favor of the community of disciples characterized the *basileia* way of life (cf. Matt 19:12).[58] Simplicity in food, drink, and clothing are recommended (Matt 6:25-34//Luke 12:22-31//*Gosp. Thom.* 36; Matt 6:11//Luke 11:3). What John Dominic Crossan calls "open commensality"—table fellowship that disregarded class, gender, and other social distinctions—was practiced (Matt 22:1-14//Luke 14:15-24//*Gosp. Thom.* 64; Matt 9:10-13; Mark 2:15-17; Luke 5:29-32).[59] A simple, serene lifestyle, dependent on divine providence, was a stated ideal (Matt 10:29-31//Luke 12:6-7).[60] Harmony within and outside the community was cultivated (Matt 5:39//Luke 6:29a).[61] Miraculous healings heralded the *basileia*.[62] While slavery is taken for granted—for example, in the parables[63]—there is no evidence that slavery was condoned by the *basileia* movement or that its early members owned slaves; rather, mutual service is a metaphor for right relationships within the community. Like (in different ways) the Essenes, Therapeutai, and Pharisees, the early *basileia* movement was concerned about the purity of Temple worship (Matt 21:12-17//Mark 11:12-17//Luke 19:45-48//John 2:13-22).[64]

As with other utopian movements, the countercultural aspects of the *basileia* made becoming what the Matthean evangelist calls "children of the kingdom" (*huioi tēs basileias*) difficult and demanding (Matt 8:12; 13:38), setting them apart from other Jews of their time as the Essenes, Therapeutae and Pharisees were separate. "The tribe of the Christians," as Josephus later called them (*Jewish Antiquties* 18.3.3), like the other utopian Jewish movements, sought divine *basileia* in their own distinctive way. Unlike the other sectarian groups, the *basileia* movement to which Jesus belonged has, as Josephus put it, endured to the present day (*Jewish Antiquities* 18.3.3).

CONCLUSION:
FROM *BASILEIA to* EKKLĒSIA

The stated purpose of this study was to bring together Jesus' teachings on the kingdom of God and ancient utopian writings in order to offer a new perspective on this central aspect of his message. Along the way, it has been shown that the proclamation of *hē basileia tou theou* was very much at home among the many utopian/eutopian traditions of antiquity, both Jewish and non-Jewish. In particular, it has been shown that the Hebrew scriptures and early Jewish writings contain many visions of an ideal society, often (but not always) identified with Israel.

There are many similarities and overlaps between Jewish and non-Jewish utopian traditions. One salient difference is that Jewish utopianism was more inclined than Graeco-Roman to be nationalistic, and, as far as we know, the earliest actual utopian communities, the Essenes and the Therapeutai, were Jewish. The *basileia* movement of Jesus' time did not form communes like these sectarian groups, but the Pharisaic *havurah* provides a comparable early Jewish effort to actualize divine rule in a noncommunal setting. Also like the *havurah*, the *basileia* was not conceived in nationalistic terms, but its members strove to live in a manner consistent with the apprehension of God's cosmic reign.

By the time the earliest extant Christian documents, the letters of Paul, were written, the martyred proclaimer of the kingdom had become the content of the proclamation.[1] The *basileia* continued to be a theme of early Christian preaching; as with other Jewish understandings of divine rule, it was interpreted in various ways by the new Jesus movement. However, the emergent church's increasing focus on Jesus rather than on the *basileia* necessitated that Jesus be proclaimed along with, or even instead of, the kingdom.[2] Paul understands the kingdom as "consummated in the future but . . . [having] already achieved anticipatory reality in the present through the resurrection and reign of Christ."[3] For Mark, the kingdom is an eschatological *mysterion* that can only be apprehended by disciples who truly see, hear, perceive, and understand the parabolic teaching and messianic identity of Jesus.[4] In Matthew, the "kingdom of heaven," presided over by the Petrine church (Matt 16:18-19), is accessible only to those who do God's will as epitomized in the Torah taught by Jesus (Matt 7:21; cf. 5:3, 10, 19, 20; 13:52; 19:12). For Luke, "Jesus is the king, and following him leads to the kingdom"; the whole gospel message can be summed up as either "Jesus" or "the kingdom."[5] The Johannine Gospel uses the phrase *hē basileia tou theou* only twice (John 3:3, 5; cf. 18:36), possibly because of its appropriation by Sethian Gnosticism to refer not to salvation but to a fleshly impediment to it.[6] In the deutero-Pauline writings, the "kingdom of light" is the "kingdom of Christ and of God" (Col 1:12-13; Eph 5:5), which grants believers a place in the "heavenly realms" with the enthroned Jesus (Eph 1:20; 2:6). For Revelation, the kingdom of God and Christ is a future promise of salvation to the saints enduring persecution for their faith (Rev 11:15; 12:10; cf. 1:6, 9; 5:10). Proto-orthodox writers of the second century construct the kingdom as "almost uniformly future . . . heavenly . . . and eternal."[7]

Although the *basileia* proclamation receded in importance in the Jesus movement, the pursuit of utopia in various guises continued.

As with the Hebrew scriptures, utopian themes pervade the writings of the earliest Christians. The book of Acts depicts the early church in Jerusalem as a harmonious commune that eschewed private property, ruled by the Spirit-filled apostles:

> Now the whole group of those who believed were of one heart and soul, and no one claimed private ownership of any possessions, but everything they owned was held in common. With great power the apostles gave their testimony to the resurrection of the Lord Jesus, and great grace was upon them all. There was not a needy person among them, for as many as owned lands or houses sold them and brought the proceeds of what was sold. They laid it at the apostles' feet, and it was distributed to each as any had need. (Acts 4:32-35)

Like the citizens of some of the hellenistic utopias described in chapter 1, those who fail to live up to the lofty standards of the community are decisively dealt with; in the case of Ananias and Sapphira, the penalty is not mere eviction but sudden death (Acts 5:5, 10). While it is doubtful that the earliest church in Jerusalem was actually organized according to these "communistic" principles, Luke's description clearly expresses "the Jewish- Christian interpretation of a Greek [utopian] ideal" with the parenetic purpose of encouraging the sharing of wealth in the Lucan community.[8]

Matthew, reminiscent of Philo and Josephus, portrays Jesus as a new Moses, a consummate lawgiver who addresses the "lost sheep of the house of Israel" from a mountain (Matthew 5–7) and delivers five sermons corresponding to the five books of Torah (Matthew 10; 13; 18; 23–25).[9] In one of only two Gospel passages to use the term *church* (*ekklēsia*; cf. Matt 16:18), Matthew's Jesus stipulates the conditions under which members are to be excommunicated:

> "If another member of the church sin against you, go and point out the fault when the two of you are alone. If the member listens to you, you have regained that one. But if

> you are not listened to, take one or two others along with
> you, so that every word may be confirmed by the evidence
> of two or three witnesses. If the member refuses to listen
> to them, tell it to the church; and if the offender refuses to
> listen even to the church, let such a one be to you as a Gen-
> tile and a tax collector. Truly I tell you, whatever you bind
> on earth will be bound in heaven, and whatever you loose
> on earth will be loosed in heaven." (Matt 18:15-17)

Dennis Duling describes the Matthean community as "a small-group 'brotherhood' led by marginal scribes with an ideology that combats status hierarchy with respect to leaders,"[10] in which there was tension and discontinuity between an egalitarian ideology and a social reality of emergent hierarchical authority structures.[11]

Hebrews portrays persecuted, struggling believers as already par-ticipating in "Mount Zion and . . . the city of the living God, the heav-enly Jerusalem, . . . and innumerable angels in festal gathering" (Heb 12:23). Similarly, the Apocalypse promises a "new heaven and the new earth" (Rev 21:1—22:5) to "holy people" able patiently to endure until its appearance (Rev 1:9; 2:3; 3:10; 13:10; 14:12). The seer's description of the reward of the persecuted saints, the new Jerusalem "prepared as a bride for her husband" (21:2), recalls the vision of Ezekiel with its "foursquare city" (Rev 21:16; Ezek 42:20; cf. Rev 22:1-2; Ezek 47:1) and the Garden of Eden with its life-giving rivers and the tree of life (Rev 22:1-2; Gen 2:9-10), lit by the primal light of creation (Rev 22:5; Gen 1:3-4). Like the idealized Temple precinct of Ezekiel, the new Jerusalem will be free of defilement, but it will need no Temple, because "the throne of God and the Lamb will be in it" (Rev 22:3). In the universalistic spirit of Third Isaiah, the leaves of the tree of life are for "the healing of the nations" (Rev 22:2).

As Everett Ferguson has noted, studies of the kingdom of God in postcanonical literature are much less numerous than those dealing with the Bible.[12] Suffice it to say, the *basileia* has been identified with the church, with Christ, with the Christian state, and with heaven itself through the millennia,[13] and it will continue to evoke a multiplicity of interpretations from those who, like Joseph of Arimathea, are looking for the kingdom of God. With such disparate evidence, it is difficult to discern to what extent the utopian elements sketched above correlated with eutopian social practices in the earliest churches; such a discussion is outside the scope of this study, as is the question of the relationship between kingdom and *ekklēsia* in the history of theology. It is tempting to use Alfred Loisy's famous observation that "Jesus foretold the kingdom, and it was the Church that came"[14] to conclude with a facile distinction between the dynamic *basileia* movement of Jesus' time and its later, Christ-worshiping and increasingly institutionalized developments. However, recent scholarship has drawn attention to the pitfalls of "the myth of Christian origins" that "there was an original moment of perfect egalitarianism, from which subsequent history is a 'fall.'"[15] It is as unlikely that the *basileia* movement of Jesus' time perfectly lived out its utopian ideals any more (or less) than did the Essenes, Therapeutai, Pharisees, or the emergent Christianities reflected in the New Testament. Utopian impulses continued into the second century, as the idealizing description of the Christian community found in the *Apology of Aristides*, addressed to the Emperor Hadrian, poignantly illustrates:

> For they know and trust in God, the Creator of heaven and of earth, in whom and from whom are all things . . . from whom they received commandments which they engraved upon their minds and observe in hope and expectation of the world which is to come. Wherefore they do not commit adultery, nor bear false witness, nor embezzle what is held in pledge, nor covet what is not theirs. They honour father and mother, and show kindness to those near to them; and whenever they are judges, they judge uprightly. They do not worship idols [made] in the image of man; and whatsoever they would not that others should do unto them, they do not to others; and of the food which is consecrated to idols they do not eat, for they are pure. And their enemies they appease . . . and make them their friends; they do good to their enemies; and their women . . . are pure as virgins, and their daughters are modest. Further, if one or

other of them have bondmen and bondwomen or children, through love towards them they persuade them to become Christians, and when they have done so, they call them brethren without distinction. . . . Falsehood is not found among them; and they love one another, and from widows they do not turn away their esteem; and they deliver the orphan from him who treats him harshly. . . . And he, who has, gives to him who has not, without boasting. And when they see a stranger, they take him in to their homes and rejoice over him as a very brother; for they do not call them brethren after the flesh, but brethren after the spirit and in God. And whenever one of their poor passes from the world, each one of them according to his ability gives heed to him and carefully sees to his burial.[16]

What Jane Schaberg describes as "a social reality characterized by the attempts of men and women to live and work together for a common goal as equals, in a variety of changing circumstances and understandings" undoubtedly was shared to some extent by both the *basileia* movement and the church that followed.[17] Further research is required fully to unpack the expressions and interrelations of kingdom, church and utopia/eutopia in emergent Christianity.

NOTES

Introduction

1. See *A Lexicon Abridged from Liddell and Scott's Greek-English Lexicon* (Oxford: Clarendon, 1977), 599.

2. *Gage Canadian Dictionary* (Toronto: Gage Learning, 1983), 1239.

3. See especially John J. Collins, "Models of Utopia in the Biblical Tradition," in *A Wise and Discerning Mind: Essays in Honor of Burke O. Long*, ed. Saul M. Olyan and Robert Culley (Providence, RI: Brown Judaic Studies, 2000), 51–57; Binyamin Uffenheimer, "Utopia and Reality in Biblical Thought," *Immanuel* 9 (1979): 1–15; Jacob Neusner, "Qumran and Jerusalem: Two Jewish Roads to Utopia," *Journal of Bible and Religion* 27 (1959): 284–90; Mary Ann Beavis, "Philo's Therapeutai: Philosopher's Dream or Utopian Construction?" *Journal for the Study of the Pseudepigrapha* 14 (2004): 30–42; Beavis, "The Kingdom of God, 'Utopia' and Theocracy," *Journal for the Study of the Historical Jesus* 2 (2004): 91–106.

4. E.g., Lewis Mumford, *The Story of Utopias* (New York: Boni and Liveright, 1922), 59–60; F. E. Manuel and F. P. Manuel, *Utopian Thought in the Western World* (Cambridge, MA: Belknap, 1979), 46–48; J. Ferguson, *Utopias in the Classical World* (Ithaca, NY: Cornell University Press, 1975), 146–55.

5. Thomas More, *Utopia*, trans. Clarence Miller (New Haven, CT: Yale University Press, 2001). The book was first published in 1516.

6. See Miller, "Introduction," *Utopia*, ix.

7. Manuel and Manuel, *Utopian Thought*, 1.

8. See Lynda H. Schneekloth, "Unredeemably Utopian: Architecture and Making/Unmaking the World," *Utopian Studies* 9 (1998): 1. See also Mary Ann Beavis, "Feminist Eutopian Visions of the City," in *Women and Urban Environments 2: Feminist Eutopian Visions of the City*, ed. Mary Ann Beavis (Winnipeg: Institute of Urban Studies, 1997), 45–61.

9. E. D. S. Sullivan, *The Utopian Vision: Seven Essays on the Quincentennial of Sir Thomas More* (San Diego, Calif.: San Diego State University Press, 1983), 6.

10. Manuel and Manuel, *Utopian Thought*, 4–5.

11. Ibid., 5.

12. Doyne Dawson, *Cities of the Gods: Communist Utopias in Greek Thought* (New York: Oxford University Press, 1992), 7.

13. Collins, "Models of Utopia."

14. Doron Mendels, "Hellenistic Utopia and the Essenes," in *Identity, Religion and Historiography: Studies in Hellenistic History*, ed. D. Mendels (JSPSup 24; Sheffield: Sheffield Academic, 1998), 420–39.

15. Neusner, "Qumran and Jerusalem."

16. Doron Mendels, *The Rise and Fall of Jewish Nationalism: Jewish and Christian Ethnicity in Ancient Palestine* (New York: Doubleday, 1982).

17. See Norman Perrin and Dennis C. Duling, *The New Testament: An Introduction* (2nd ed.: New York: Harcourt Brace Jovanovich, 1982), 405–6. Perrin's criteria are dissimilarity, multiple attestation, and coherence; R. H. Fuller's are distinctiveness, the cross-section

method, consistency and linguistic and environmental tests. Perrin notes that he and Fuller, working apart, arrived at "virtually identical conclusions" (405).

18. See Robert W. Funk, Roy W. Hoover, and the Jesus Seminar, *The Five Gospels: What Did Jesus Really Say?* (New York: Macmillan, 1993); and Robert W. Funk and the Jesus Seminar, *The Acts of Jesus: The Search for the Authentic Deeds of Jesus* (San Francisco: HarperSanFrancisco, 1998). For critique and response, see, e.g., Robert J. Miller, *The Jesus Seminar and Its Critics* (Santa Rosa, CA: Polebridge, 1999). See also Stanley E. Porter, *The Criteria for Authenticity in Historical-Jesus Research: Previous Discussion and New Proposals* (JSNTSup 191; Sheffield: Sheffield Academic, 2000); and William R. Herzog, *Jesus, Justice, and the Reign of God: A Ministry of Liberation* (Louisville, KY: Westminster John Knox, 2000), 38–42.

19. Richard A. Horsley and Neil Asher Silberman, *The Message and the Kingdom: How Jesus and Paul Ignited a Revolution and Transformed the Ancient World* (Minneapolis: Fortress Press, 2004).

20. Dieter Georgi, "The Interest in the Life of Jesus Theology as a Paradigm for the Social History of Biblical Criticism," *Harvard Theological Review* 85 (1992): 52–83.

21. Elisabeth Schüssler Fiorenza, *Jesus and the Politics of Interpretation* (New York: Continuum, 2000), 43.

22. See, e.g., Schüssler Fiorenza, *Jesus and Politics*, 48–51; building on Mary Rose D'Angelo's argument that Jesus should be considered as part of a larger movement rather than as its leader ("Re-membering Jesus: Women, Prophecy, and Resistance in the Memory of the Early Churches," *Horizons* 19 [1992]: 199–218).

23. Paula Fredriksen, *Jesus of Nazareth: King of the Jews* (New York: Vintage, 2000), 268.

24. John P. Meier, *A Marginal Jew: Reconsidering the Historical Jesus, Volume 2: Mentor, Message, Miracles* (New York: Doubleday, 1994), 4.

CHAPTER 1

1. Dawson, *Cities of the Gods*, 7. Dawson does not specify what he means by his reference to "messianic works" in the Greek tradition.

2. Similar accounts of the ages and races of the world are referred to in Plato, *The Statesman* 268e–274d; Aratus of Soli, *Phaenomena* 96–136; Diodorus Siculus 5.66.1–4; Virgil, *Eclogues* 4.4 and *Georgics* 1.125; 2.336, 532; *Aeneid* 8.313; Dionysius of Halicarnassus 1.36.1; Propertius, *Elegies* 2.32.49; Ovid, *Metamorphoses* 1.89–150, 15.96ff.; *Amores* 3.8.35; *Fasti* 4.395; Seneca, *Hippolytus* 525ff.; Statius, *Silvae* 1.4.2, 1.6.39–50; Hyginus, *Astronomica* 2.25; Aelian, *Varia Historica* 3.18; and Boethius, *The Consolation of Philosophy* 2.5. "The four-fold pattern of kingdoms appears also in *Sibylline Oracles* 4, Babylonian and Greek writings, and Qumran scrolls (4QpseudoDan)" (*The New Oxford Annotated Bible, New Revised Version with the Apocrypha,* ed. Michael D. Coogan [3rd ed.; Oxford: Oxford University Press, 2001], 1258nn33–44); and in the Zoroastrian *Bahman Yasht* (*Oxford Annotated Bible,* 1257nn32–33; see also 2 Esdr 7:55–56). For discussion, see F. E. Manuel and F. P. Manuel, *Utopian Thought,* 64–75.

3. See "Saturnus, Saturnalia," in *The Oxford Dictionary of Classical Myth and Religion,* ed. Simon Price and Emily Kearns (Oxford: Oxford University Press, 2003), 495–96.

4. Virgil, *Eclogue IV,* in *Virgil I: Eclogues, Georgics, Aeneid 1–6,* ed. H. Rushton Fairclough (rev. ed.; LCL; Cambridge: Harvard University Press, 1999), 49–53.

5. John Dominic Crossan, *The Historical Jesus: The Life of a Mediterranean Jewish Peasant* (San Francisco: HarperSanFrancisco, 1992), 42; see also 38–41. For a more sympathetic appraisal of the Roman religious context of the work, see Stephen Benko, "Some Thoughts on the Fourth Eclogue," *Perspectives in Religious Studies* 2 (1975): 125–45. For Paul's construction of *hē basileia tou theou* as in deliberate opposition to the Golden Age ideology of the Roman Empire, see John Dominic Crossan and Jonathan L. Reed, *In Search of Paul: How Jesus's Apostle Opposed Rome's Empire with God's Kingdom* (San Francisco: HarperSanFrancisco, 2004).

6. Homer, *The Odyssey,* trans. E. V. Rieu (London: Penguin, 1991), 61.

7. On Orphic religion, see Larry J. Alderink, "Orphism," in *ABD* 5, 48–50.

8. According to Plutarch's account in *Moralia: Letter to Appollonius* 35,120c.

9. Manuel and Manuel, *Utopian Thought*, 77 (quoting Pindar, *Works* [trans. Lewis Richard Farnell; London: Macmillan, 1930], 333, frag. 129).

10. Manuel and Manuel, *Utopian Thought*, 77, quoting Plato, *Republic* 1.131. Both Plato and Cicero (106–43 BCE) located the blessed realm in the heavens above the stars (Colleen McDannell and Bernhard Lange, *Heaven: A History* [New Haven: Yale University Press, 2001], 16; see Plato, *Phaedrus* 246E–249D and Cicero, *On the Republic* 6.9–26 (*Scipio's Dream*).

11. See discussion in Manuel and Manuel, *Utopian Thought*, 77–78.

12. For another account of Plato's Atlantis, see John Ferguson, *Utopias of the Classical World* (Aspects of Greek and Roman Life; Ithaca, NY: Cornell University Press, 1975), 73–74.

13. For fuller accounts of hellenistic utopian romances, see Ferguson, *Utopias*, 102–10, 122–29; Manuel and Manuel, *Utopian Thought*, 81–92.

14. For summaries of Euhemerus's account of Panchaïa, see Ferguson, *Utopias*, 104–8; Manuel and Manuel, *Utopian Thought*, 87–90.

15. Euhemerus is the philosopher famous for his opinion that the gods are really human beings of the past, deified by subsequent generations for their benefactions to humankind (see Manuel and Manuel, *Utopian Thought*, 85–86, 89–90). A recent and authoritative work on his career is M. Winiarczyk, *Euhemeros von Messene: Leben, Werk und Nachwirkung. Beiträge zur Altertumskunde, Band 157* (Munich: K. G. Saur, 2002).

16. Preserved only in excerpts in Diodorus Siculus (5.41–46) and Lactantius, *Divine Institutes* 13. Utopian scholars are divided as to whether Euhemerus's tale of Panchaïa is a mere novel (Manuel and Manuel, *Utopian Thought*, 87–90) or written with serious philosophical intent (Ferguson, *Utopias*, 104–8).

17. On Hippodamus, see Dawson, *Cities of the Gods*, 21–26, 29–31.

18. Manuel and Manuel, *Utopian Thought*, 89.

19. Ibid.

20. Mentioned by Josephus as a contemporary of Alexander the

Great who lived in the court of Ptolemy I of Egypt (*Against Apion* 1.22.183–205; *Jewish Antiquities* 1.7.2).

21. For a fuller summary, see Manuel and Manuel, *Utopian Thought*, 84–86; see also James S. Romm, *The Edges of the Earth in Ancient Thought: Geography, Exploration, and Fiction* (Princeton, NJ: Princeton University Press, 1992), 60–67.

22. *Diodorus Siculus II*, trans. C. H. Oldfather (LCL; Cambridge: Harvard University Press; London: William Heinemann, 1935), 41. All quotations from Diodorus are from this edition.

23. Based on Aelian, *De natura animalium* 11, quoted in Manuel and Manuel, *Utopian Thought*, 85.

24. Manuel and Manuel, *Utopian Thought*, 86, citing Pomponius's *De chorographia* 3.

25. Pliny, *Natural History*, 2.4 (quoted in Manuel and Manuel, *Utopian Thought*, 86).

26. Romm, *Edges of the Earth*, 51.

27. A miraculous "Table of the Sun" produces all kinds of cooked meats (ibid., 56, 58).

28. Ibid., 57.

29. Ibid., 58.

30. Ibid.

31. Ibid.

32. For other summaries of Iambulus, see Manuel and Manuel, *Utopian Thought*, 86–87, and Ferguson, *Utopias*, 127–29; see also D. Wilson, "Iambulus' Islands of the Sun and Hellenistic Literary Utopias," *Science Fiction Studies* 10, no. 3 (November 1976), http://www.depauw.edu/sfs/backissues/10/winston10art.htm.

33. Dawson, *Cities of the Gods*, 7.

34. Ibid.. Other examples of low utopias are Plato's *Laws*, Aristotle's *Politics* 7–8, and *On the Republic* and *On the Laws* by Cicero.

35. Slaves are not mentioned, although they may be simply assumed to be present.

36. Ferguson, *Utopias*, 66, notes that the laborers as well as guardians/rulers would have to receive the same education for class mobility to be feasible.

37. See Plato, *Republic* (Harmondsworth, Middlesex: Penguin, 1955), 243–44n3.

38. On the question of Plato's "feminism," see Dawson, *Cities of the Gods*, 88–89.

39. Ibid. Ferguson opines that the entirety of the ideal state proposed in the *Republic* was not intended "to be thought of as an actuality or even as a practical possibility, although he no doubt wished it might be" (*Utopias*, 68).

40. Ibid.

41. Ferguson, *Utopias*, 67.

42. See Dawson, *Cities of the Gods*, 93–95.

43. Translation by Benjamin Jowett, *Aristotle's Politics* (Oxford: Clarendon, 1920).

44. See Dawson, *Cities of the Gods*, 111–222.

45. Ibid., 97–98.

46. To which the eighth book of the *Politics* is solely devoted.

47. Aristotle considers abortion to be preferable to exposure, which is resorted to only in the case of deformed infants.

48. Dawson, *Cities of the Gods*, 98.

49. As Dawson notes, "The word *oikos* [household] implied both family and property" (ibid., 134).

50. See the discussion of woman's distinctive nature in *Politics* 1.13.

51. Although on a pragmatic level, it was recognized that a wise man should marry and have children (see Dawson, *Cities of the Gods*, 190–91), "relations with wives and even mistresses should be based on friendship" (193).

52. See ibid., 134–37, 183–84, 190–93. On Stoic attitudes toward women, see W. Klassen, "Musonius Rufus, Jesus and Paul: Three First-Century Feminists," in *From Jesus to Paul: Studies in Honour of Francis Wright Beare*, edited by P. Richardson and J. C. Hurd (Waterloo, ON: Wilfrid Laurier University Press),185–206; C. E. Manning, "Seneca and the Stoics on the Equality of the Sexes," *Mnemosyne* ser. 4, 26 (1973): 170–77.

53. Dawson, *Cities of the Gods*, 38.

54. See ibid., 37.

55. Ferguson, *Utopias*, 65.

56. Dawson, *Cities of the Gods*, 40.

57. Ibid.

58. On ancient Greek women philosophers, see *A History of Women Philosophers, Volume 1: 600 B.C.–500 A.D.*, ed. Mary Ellen Waithe (Dordrecht: Martinus Nijhoff, 1987), 11–116, 197–209.

59. Two possibilities would be Perictyone I—possibly the mother of Plato—and Axiothea of Philesia; see ibid., 1:60–71, 205–6.

60. See Ferguson, *Utopias*, 29–39; Dawson, *Cities of the Gods*, 21–36; and especially Elizabeth Rawson, *The Spartan Tradition in European Thought* (Oxford: Clarendon, 1969), 12–115.

61. See Rawson, *Spartan Tradition*, 171.

62. Ferguson, *Utopias*, 29; Manuel and Manuel, *Utopian Thought*, 97–99; Dawson, *Cities of the Gods*, 26–37.

63. See Ferguson, *Utopias*, 126–27.

64. Solon and Zaleucus Locrensis are also mentioned by Josephus as legislators much admired by the Greeks (*Against Apion* 2.154).

65. See Ferguson, *Utopias*, 42–45.

66. Ibid., 45.

67. See Manuel and Manuel, *Utopian Thought*, 94–96.

68. Translation in Thucydides, *The History of the Peloponnesian War*, trans. Richard Crawley (London: Dent; New York: Dutton, 1945).

69. Plutarch, "Solon," *Lives*, trans Bernadotte Perrin (LCL; London: William Heinemann, 1914), 453.

70. Manuel and Manuel, *Utopian Thought*, 94.

71. See ibid., 94, 96–97.

72. Dawson, *Cities of the Gods*, 14.

73. Ibid., 14–15.

74. Ibid., 17.

75. Ibid.

76. Ibid., 18.

77. Ferguson, *Utopias*, 107.

78. Ibid.

79. Ibid., 110.

80. Ferguson, *Utopias*, 110.

CHAPTER 2

1. Two exceptions are Uffenheimer, "Utopia and Reality," 1–15; and Collins, "Models of Utopia," 51–67.

2. Uffenheimer, "Utopia and Reality," 2.

3. Collins, "Models of Utopia," 51–52. See Jonanathan Z. Smith, *Map Is Not Territory: Studies in the History of Religions* (Chicago/London: University of Chicago Press, 1978), xii, 100–103, 130–42, 147–51, 160–66, 169–71, 185–89, 291–94, 308–9.

4. Collins, "Models of Utopia," 52.

5. Ibid.

6. Norman Perrin, "Jesus and the Language of the Kingdom," in *The Kingdom of God*, ed. Bruce Chilton (Philadelphia: Fortress Press; London: SPCK, 1984), 94; italics in original.

7. Collins, "Models of Utopia," 51.

8. Jean Delumeau, *History of Paradise: The Garden of Eden in Myth and Tradition* (New York: Continuum, 1995); T. Stordalen, *Echoes of Eden: Genesis 2–3 and Symbolism of the Eden Garden in Biblical Hebrew Literature* (CBET 25; Leuven: Peeters, 2000); H. N. Wallace, *The Eden Narrative* (HSM 32; Atlanta: Scholars, 1985); James Barr, *The Garden of Eden and the Hope of Immortality* (Minneapolis: Fortress Press, 1993); Beverly J. Stratton, *Out of Eden: Reading, Rhetoric, and Ideology in Genesis 2–3* (Sheffield: Academic, 1995); Paul and Deborah Morris, *A Walk in the Garden: Biblical, Iconographical and Literary Images of Eden* (Sheffield: Sheffield Academic, 1992); see also Jeffrey Burton Russell, *A History of Heaven: The Singing Silence* (Princeton, NJ: Princeton University Press, 1997).

9. As Collins notes ("Models of Utopia," 52).

10. See A. R. Millard, "The Etymology of Eden," *Vetus Testamentum* 34, no. 1 (1984): 103–5. See also W. F. Albright, "Primitivism in Ancient Western Asia," in *Primitivism and Related Ideas in Antiquity*, by Arthur O. Lovejoy and George Boas, with supplementary essays by W. F. Albright and P. E. Dumont (New York: Octagon, 1935), 424–25.

11. Samuel Noah Kramer, *Sumerian Mythology: A Study of Spiritual and Literary Achievement in the Third Millennium, B.C.* (Philadelphia: University of Pennsylvania Press, 1972), 55.

12. Delumeau, *History of Paradise*, 5; cf. Collins, "Models of Utopia," 52–53.

13. Stordalen, *Echoes of Eden*, chs. 12–14.

14. See *1 Enoch* 32:2–4; 60:8, 23; 61:12; 70:4); Fragment 3 from *Sibylline Oracles*, cited in Theophylus, *To Autolycus* 2.36; *Apocalypse of Moses* 28:4; 6:2; 9:3; 13:1–4; 40:6; *3 Apoc. Bar.* 4:10.

15. R. Rubinkiewicz, trans., "Apocalypse of Abraham," in *The Old Testament Pseudepigrapha*, ed. James H. Charlesworth (Garden City, NY: Doubleday, 1983), 1:699.

16. *T. Ab.* [A] 11:1, 10; *2 Apoc. Bar.* 4:6; 51:7-11; *Life of Adam and Eve* 25:3; 42:4; *Apoc. Mos.* 2:6; 37:5; 40:1; 2 Cor 12:2-3; *2 Enoch* [A] 8:1—9:1.

17. *T. Dan* 5:12; Luke 23:43; Rev 2:7; 22:2, 14, 18; *Apoc. Sedr.* 12:2; 16:6; [Vulgate] Ecclus. [Sir] 44:16. I am indebted to James L. Kugel, *The Bible As It Was* (Cambridge: Harvard University Press, 1997), 79–82, for the references in notes 15–17.

18. H. C. Kee, trans., "Testaments of the Twelve Patriarchs," in Charlesworth, ed., *Pseudepigrapha*, 1:775–828.

19. See Russell, *History of Heaven*, 33–39, 42–44.

20. Collins, "Models of Utopia," 65–66.

21. Ibid., 51–52, citing the opinion of Claus Westermann that "all attempts to explain or locate the sources of the four rivers geographically are ruled out" (*Genesis 1–11* [Continental Commentaries; Minneapolis: Augsburg, 1984], 216). For attempts to locate *Gan Eden* geographically, see W. Creighton Marlow, "Eden," *Eerdmans Dictionary of the Bible*, ed. David Noel Freedman (Grand Rapids: Eerdmans, 2000), 371.

22. Note that Iambulus and his companion are ejected from the Islands of the Sun when they begin to do evil.

23. Joseph F. Wimmer, "Promise," in Freedman, ed., *Eerdmans Dictionary of the Bible*, 1085.

24. W. G. Plaut, *The Torah: A Modern Commentary* (New York: Union of American Hebrew Congregations, 1981), 100.

25. Plaut notes that "some commentators deny the Abrahamic antiquity of the tradition and claim that it arose in later ages to give the

military conquest of the land by Joshua an *ex post facto* religious legitimation. Even if this were so, it would emphasize that for Abraham's descendants military acquisition and physical possession—sufficient for all other nations' claims—were not the core of their relationship to the land" (ibid., 100).

26. For the translation of the verb *zb* as "exuding" or "oozing," see Etan Levine, "The Land of Milk and Honey," *Journal for the Study of the Old Testament* 87 (2000): 43n2.

27. Ibid., 44.

28. Ibid.

29. Ibid., 49–52.

30. Ibid., 49.

31. Ibid.

32. Ibid.

33. B. W. Anderson, "Exodus Typology in Second Isaiah," in *Israel's Prophetic Heritage: Essays in Honor of James Muilenburg*, ed. B. W. Anderson and W. Harrelson (New York: Harper & Row, 1962), 177–95.

34. On the land as gift and temptation, see Walter Brueggemann, *The Land: Place as Gift, Promise, and Challenge in Biblical Faith* (Overtures to Biblical Theology; Philadelphia: Fortress, 1977), 47–59.

35. Collins, "Models of Utopia," 53.

36. Ibid.

37. Ibid.

38. On the reign of Solomon as a "golden age" of Israel, see David Jobling, "'Forced Labor': Solomon's Golden Age and the Question of Literary Representation," *Semeia* 54 (1991): 57–76.

39. See Shemaryahu Talmon, *King, Cult, and Calendar in Ancient Israel: Collected Studies* (Jerusalem: Magnes, 1986), 145.

40. Ibid., 144.

41. Ibid., 161.

42. R. B. Wright, "Psalms of Solomon," in Charlesworth, ed., *Old Testament Pseudepigrapha*, 2:667.

43. Ibid., 645.

44. Ibid.

45. Ibid., 54.

46. Ibid.

47. Ibid. In the second century BCE apocalypse *1 Enoch,* the "holy mountain" is located in the center of the earth (26:1). On the Greek concept of Delphi as the navel of the earth, see James S. Romm, *The Edges of the Earth in Ancient Thought* (Princeton, NJ: Princeton University Press, 1992), 65.

48. Collins, "Models of Utopia," 54.

49. Ibid., 55.

50. Ibid., 56.

51. See ibid.

52. Ibid., 58.

53. Ibid. Collins notes that the utopian vision of *Sib. Or.* 3:788–95 shows remarkable parallels with Virgil's Fourth Eclogue, which evokes the Sibyl of Cumae: "Whether Virgil was acquainted with Isaiah or with the Jewish sibyl has long been disputed, but never conclusively shown" (59); see also John J. Collins, "The Jewish Transformation of the Sibylline Oracles," in *Seers, Sibyls and Sages in Hellenistic-Roman Judaism* (Leiden: Brill, 1997), 192–97.

54. For a discussion of the possible geographical referents of the biblical maps, see Walter C. Kaiser Jr., "The Promised Land: A Biblical-Historical View," *Bibliotheca Sacra* 138 (1981): 302–12.

55. See Michael D. Coogan, ed., *The New Annotated Oxford Bible, New Revised Version with the Apocrypha* (3rd ed.; Oxford: Oxford University Press, 2001), 236, note on 34:1-28; see also James W. Flanagan, "The Deuteronomic Meaning of the Phrase '*kol yiśrā'ēl*,'" *Studies in Religion* 6 (1976–77): 166.

56. See Kaiser, "Promised Land," 305–6.

57. For explanations of the discrepancies among the various "maps" of Israel delineated in the Hebrew Bible, see W. Janzen, "Land," in *ABD* 4:146; see also Flanagan, "Deuteronomic Meaning."

58. Menahem Haran, *Temples and Temple-Service in Ancient Israel* (Oxford: Clarendon, 1978), 122.

59. Uffenheimer, "Utopia and Reality," 2.

60. Ibid., 3.

61. Ibid., 3–15; Collins, "Models of Utopia," 53. The etymology of the term *jubilee* is obscure; the word *yôbēl* may refer to the trumpet

that initiates the festival year, but it may also be related to the root *ybl*, referring to liberation (Sharon H. Ringe, *Jesus, Liberation, and the Biblical Jubilee* [Overtures to Biblical Theology; Philadelphia: Fortress Press, 1985], 24–25).

62. Uffenheimer, "Utopia and Reality," 4–5.

63. Robin J. DeWitt Knauth, "Jubilee, Year of," in Freedman, ed., *Eerdmans Dictionary of the Bible*, 743.

64. Ringe, *Biblical Jubilee*, 16.

65. E.g., ibid.; Uffenheimer, "Utopia and Reality," 5; Israel Knohl, *The Sanctuary of Silence: The Priestly Torah and the Holiness School* (Minneapolis: Fortress Press, 1995), 217; Christopher J. H. Wright, "Jubilee, Year of," in *ABD* 3:1028–29.

66. Robert S. Kawashima, "The Jubilee Year and the Return of Cosmic Purity," *Catholic Biblical Quarterly* 65 (2005): 371.

67. Ibid., 386.

68. Ibid., 371–72.

69. See Wright, "Jubilee," 1028.

70. Cf. Ringe, *Biblical Jubilee*, 29. On jubilee imagery in the New Testament, see Ringe, *Biblical Jubilee*, 33–90.

71. See O. S. Wintermute, "Jubilees," in Charlesworth, ed., *Old Testament Pseudepigrapha*, 2:39.

72. Ibid., citing M. Testuz, *Les Idées religieuses du livre des Jubilés* (Geneva: Librairie E. Droz, 1960), 138–40, and E. Weisenberg, "The Jubilee of Jubilees," *Restoration Quarterly* 3 (1961/1962): 3–40.

73. Ibid.

74. Ibid., 100.

75. F. H. Colson, trans., *Philo* IV (LCL; Cambridge: Harvard; London: William Heinemann, 1984), 457. All subsequent quotations of the *Life of Moses* will be from this translation.

76. See Louis H. Feldman, "Josephus' Portrait of Moses, Part Three," *Jewish Quarterly Review* 83 (1993): 313–20.

77. Norman Perrin, *Jesus and the Language of the Kingdom* (Philadelphia: Fortress Press, 1976), 16–17.

78. Ibid., 17.

79. Ibid. See also Num 23:21; Jer 8:19; 10:10; 46:18; 48:15; Zeph 3:15; 14:9, 16-17; Mal 1:14.

80. Perrin, *Jesus*, 18.

81. Ibid.

82. Ibid., 18–20.

83. Ibid., 20.

84. Ibid., 81n9, concedes that the phrase "the kingdom of God" may be an early Christian expression; in ancient Judaism, the tendency is to use the noun "kingdom" with a personal pronoun referring to God ("his kingdom"), or to speak of God reigning or being king.

85. Ibid., 21.

86. Ibid., 22.

87. Ibid., quoting Philip Wheelwright's citation of Alan Watts.

88. Ibid., 24.

89. Ibid., 24–25.

90. Translation in ibid., 26–27. Cf. Dan 2:44; 4:34.

91. Ibid., 27.

92. Ibid., 31.

93. Ibid., 29–32, following Philip Wheelwright and Paul Ricoeur. Perrin conceded that it is not always easy to make the distinction between tensive and steno-symbols and that each usage of the symbolism of the kingdom of God must be considered on its merits (31).

94. See also Num 23:21; Pss 24:10; 89:18; 98:6; 103:19; Jer 10:10; 46:18; 48:15; Dan 2:44; 4:34; 5:21; 6:26; Zeph 3:15; Zech 14:9, 16, 17; Mal 1:14.

CHAPTER 3

1. This chapter is a heavily revised and expanded version of my article "Philo's Therapeutai: Philosopher's Dream or Utopian Construction?" *Journal for the Study of the Pseudepigrapha* 14 (2004): 30–42.

2. On the Essenes as utopian community, see Jacob Neusner, "Qumran and Jerusalem: Two Jewish Roads to Utopia," *Journal of Bible and Religion* 27 (1959): 284–90; Collins, "Models of Utopia," 63–65; Mendels, "Hellenistic Utopia and the Essenes," in *Identity, Religion and Historiography: Studies in Hellenistic History*, edited by D. Mendels (JSPSup 24; Sheffield: Sheffield Academic, 1998), 420–39.

3. Neusner, "Qumran and Jerusalem."

4. See, e.g., Robert Eisenman and Michael Wise, *The Dead Sea Scrolls Uncovered* (New York: Penguin, 1992); Gabriel Boccaccini, *Beyond the Essene Hypothesis: The Parting of the Ways between Qumran and Enochic Judaism* (Grand Rapids: Eerdmans, 1998); Hershel Shanks, "Searching for Essenes at Ein Gedi, Not Qumran," *Biblical Archaeology Review* (July/August 2002): 90–100.

5. Since the secondhand descriptions by Philo, Josephus, and Pliny refer explicitly to the Essenes, they will be featured most prominently in the discussion below, supplemented by the (less certain) evidence from the scrolls.

6. In *Every Good Person* 76, Philo asserts that the Essenes avoid cities, but in *Hypothetica*, he mentions that they live in "many cities and villages" (11.1). For translation, see F. H. Colson, trans., *Philo* IX (LCL; Cambridge: Harvard University Press; London: William Heinemann, 1985).

7. Josephus, unlike Pliny and Philo, mentions one order of Essenes whose members marry and have women among them (*War* 11.14).

8. Collins, "Models of Utopia," 59.

9. Collins, "Models of Utopia," 59–60. On the influence of hellenistic city planning, see M. Broshi, "Visionary Architecture and Town Planning in the Dead Sea Scrolls," in *Time to Prepare the Way in the Wilderness: Papers on the Dead Sea Scrolls*, ed. D. Dimant and L. H. Schiffman (Leiden: Brill, 1995), 9–22.

10. Ibid., 60.

11. Ibid.

12. Ibid., 60–61.

13. Ibid., 61.

14. Ibid., 62.

15. Ibid.

16. Ibid., 63.

17. Translation in Geza Vermes, *The Complete Dead Sea Scrolls in English* (New York: Allen Lane/Penguin, 1997).

18. See Collins, "Models of Utopia," 64; J. Murphy-O'Connor, "La genèse littéraire de la Règle de la Communauté," *Revue Biblique* 76 (1979): 531.

19. On similarities between the Essenes and Pythagorean brotherhoods, see Moses Hadas, *Hellenistic Culture: Fusion and Diffusion* (New York: Columbia University Press, 1959), 194–96, 218.

20. Mendels, "Hellenistic Utopia," 423.

21. Ibid., 424–36.

22. Mendels, like the majority of DSS scholars, attributes their origin to the Essenes ("Hellenistic Utopia," 421n6).

23. Ibid., 436–37.

24. Translation in *Josephus: The Jewish War, Books I–III*, ed. H. St. J. Thackeray (LCL 2; Cambridge: Harvard University Press; London: William Heinemann, 1976).

25. Translation in *Josephus: The Life, Against Apion*, ed. H. St. J. Thackeray (LCL 1; Cambridge: Harvard University Press; London: William Heinemann, 1976).

26. Philo uses both the masculine (*Therapeutai*) and feminine (*Therapeutrides*) forms of the name, since the community accepted both male and female members.

27. A fuller description of the community will be given below.

28. Troels Engberg-Pedersen, "Philo's *De Vita Contemplativa* as a Philosopher's Dream," *JSJ* 30 (1999): 40–61; for a recent article that presupposes the historical existence of an Egyptian Jewish monastic community on the shores of Lake Mareotis much as described by Philo, see J. Taylor and P. R. Davies, "The So-called Therapeutai of 'De Vita contemplativa': Identity and Character," *HTR* 91 (1998): 3–24.

29. Engberg-Pedersen, "Philosopher's Dream," 48.

30. Ibid.

31. Ibid., 44–48.

32. Ibid., 46.

33. References to Philo refer to Colson, ed., *Philo*.

34. As argued by Engberg-Pedersen, "Philosopher's Dream," 42; for an argument that Philo's reference in *Life* 1 is to *Every Good Person*, see Taylor and Davies, "Therapeutai," 8–10.

35. Although, as Taylor and Davies point out, Therapeutai/Therapeutrides is not the actual name of the group described by Philo ("Therapeutai," 4–10), but a general term used by Philo to denote a certain class of philosophers, for the sake of convenience, I shall use

this terminology to refer to them. As Taylor and Davies note, many scholars have assumed that the Therapeutai were a group of Egyptian Essenes or related to the Essenes in some way (see Taylor and Davies, "Therapeutai," 3n1), a position they refute in their article.

36. Engberg-Pedersen, "Philosopher's Dream," 43.

37. On the possible location of the community, see Taylor and Davies, "Therapeutai," 10–14.

38. Engberg-Pedersen, "Philosopher's Dream," 46.

39. Taylor and Davies, "Therapeutai," 24.

40. For brief mentions of hellenistic utopian elements in Philo, see Ferguson, *Utopias*, 22, 116.

41. Although there are many similarities between the Egyptian commune and other hellenistic utopian romances, I shall focus on Diodorus's account of the Heliopolitans because it is one of the longest and most detailed examples.

42. All references to Diodorus Siculus are to Oldfather, *Diodorus*.

43. Taylor and Davies ("Therapeutai," 5) note that the term *therapeutai* was used in Greek literature, especially in Egypt, to refer to those who serve the gods; Philo goes on to mention that the term has the sense of worship (*Life* 3).

44. Ibid., 20–23.

45. Although Taylor and Davies surmise that the Therapeutai emanated from a small, elite, educated circle of Alexandrian Jews would support this suggestion ("Therapeutai," 24).

46. Engberg-Pedersen, "Philosopher's Dream," 48.

47. The term *alētheia* has the sense of both "truth" and "reality" (BDAG, 42–43).

48. Neusner, "Qumran and Jerusalem," 286. Since both Philo and Josephus agree that the Essenes lived in villages and towns scattered throughout the land, and the identification of the Essenes with the "community" of the Dead Sea Scrolls is uncertain, the Essenes' communal lifestyle is less certain.

49. Ibid., 285.

50. Ibid.

51. Ibid., 286. Cf. Josephus's assertion that he had followed the Pharisaic example by involving himself in the life of the *polis* after his three-year sojourn with the desert sage Banus (Josephus, *Life* 12).

52. Neusner, "Qumran and Jerusalem" 285.

53. Ibid., 286.

54. Ibid., 287.

55. Ibid., 288. A more detailed account of the initiation process is given on the same page. The ancient source for the initiation is the Tosefta (*t. Demai* 2); see Tal Ilan, "Paul and Pharisee Women," in *On the Cutting Edge: The Study of Women in Biblical Worlds*, ed. Jane Schaberg, Alice Bach, and Esther Fuchs (New York: Continuum, 2004), 86. Tosefta is a compilation of legal rulings and traditions discarded or rejected by the Mishnah, the official Jewish second canon (Ilan, "Pharisee Women," 88).

56. Neusner, "Qumran and Jerusalem," 287; Aharon Oppenheimer, *The 'Am Ha-Aretz: A Study in the Social History of the Jewish People in the Hellenistic-Roman Period*, trans. I. H. Levine (Leiden: Brill, 1977), 119.

57. Ilan, "Pharisee Women," 87–92.

58. Ibid., 87. Cf. the Gospels, where the Pharisees are usually cast as opponents of Jesus. Josephus, however, does not use the term *Pharisees* in a pejorative way (*Jewish Antiquities* 13.10.5; *War* 2.119, 166).

59. Ibid., 88–92. Note Josephus's observation that the Pharisees are "friendly" (*philalēlloi*) toward one another (*War* 2.166).

CHAPTER 4

1. Bruce Chilton observes that the centrality of the kingdom to Jesus' message is "recognized by everyone from the first disciples of Jesus to the most skeptical of scholars" (*Pure Kingdom: Jesus' Vision of God* [Grand Rapids: Eerdmans, 1996], ix).

2. This chapter and the next are based on my "The Kingdom of God, 'Utopia' and Theocracy," *Journal for the Study of the Historical Jesus* 2 (2004): 91–106, heavily revised and expanded.

3. Since this section summarizes material that has been analyzed at length by many other scholars, it is highly dependent on surveys of the academic literature on the kingdom of God, especially D. C. Duling's comprehensive article in the *Anchor Bible Dictionary* (D. C. Duling, "Kingdom of God, Kingdom of Heaven," *ABD*, 4:49–69). For other surveys, see Chilton, *Pure Kingdom*, 1–22; Bruce Chilton, "The Kingdom of God in Recent Discussion," in *Studying the Historical Jesus: Evaluations of the State of Current Research*, ed. Bruce Chilton

and C. A. Evans (Leiden: Brill, 1994), 255–80; Bruce Chilton, "Introduction," in *The Kingdom of God*, ed. Bruce Chilton (Philadelphia: Fortress Press; London: SPCK, 1984), 1–26; Wendell Willis, ed., *The Kingdom of God in Twentieth-Century Interpretation* (Peabody, MA: Hendrickson, 1987).

4. Duling, "Kingdom of God," 50.

5. Ibid.

6. Roy A. Harrisville, "In Search of the Meaning of 'The Kingdom of God,'" *Interpretation* 47 (2004): 142. Harrisville includes the Matthean "kingdom of heaven," the substantive "kingdom," and phrases such as "kingdom of Christ" in his enumeration (see "Meaning," 140).

7. Ibid., 142.

8. Ibid., 143.

9. Ibid.

10. Ibid., 143.

11. Ibid., 144.

12. Ibid.

13. Ibid.; for New Testament references, see 151n13.

14. Ibid., 145.

15. Ibid.

16. Ibid., 145–46.

17. Ibid., 145.

18. The criteria for gauging the authenticity of the sayings of Jesus will be discussed in the next chapter.

19. See James Luther Mays, "The Language of the Reign of God," *Interpretation* 47 (2004): 117–26; Chilton, *Pure Kingdom*, 31–44.

20. See the survey in Duling, "Kingdom of God," 50–56. See also Chilton, *Pure Kingdom*, 23–31.

21. E.g., Dan 7:13-14; *Jub.* 1:28; *Pss. Sol.* 17:1–3; *T. Mos.* 10:1, 3; 1QM 6.6; 12.3, 16; 19.8 (see Duling, "Kingdom of God," 50–52).

22. Duling, "Kingdom of God," 52–52; M. Weinfeld, "Expectations of the Divine Kingdom in Biblical and Postbiblical Literature," in *Eschatology in the Bible and Christian Tradition*, ed. H. Graf Reventlow (JSOTSup 243; Sheffield: Sheffield Academic, 1997), 218–31.

23. E.g., *Sipre Leviticus* 20:26; *Sipre Deuteronomy* 20:26; *Qiddushin* 59b; *Berakhot* 2:2 (Duling, "Kingdom of God," 53).

24. Duling, "Kingdom of God," 55.

25. Ibid., 56–57.

26. Chilton, *Pure Kingdom*, 23–31.

27. Ibid., 28.

28. Ibid.

29. Ibid., 28–29.

30. Ibid., 29; italics added.

31. A point made by Chilton, *Pure Kingdom*, 30.

32. For a fuller discussion, see Chilton, "Kingdom of God," 255–80; see also his *Pure Kingdom*, 1–22, and "Introduction," 4–26; and Scot McKnight, *A New Vision For Israel: The Teachings of Jesus in National Context* (Grand Rapids: Eerdmans, 1999), 71–84.

33. Johannes Weiss, *Jesus' Proclamation of the Kingdom of God*, trans. H. Hiers and D. L. Holland (Philadelphia: Fortress Press, 1971); Albert Schweitzer, *The Quest of the Historical Jesus*, trans. R. Montgomery (London: Black, 1910).

34. See Chilton's summary of Schweitzer's contribution in *Pure Kingdom*, 1–3.

35. C. H. Dodd, T*he Parables of the Kingdom* (London: Nisbet, 1935).

36. Chilton, *Pure Kingdom*, 7.

37. A recent, and very different, denial of futuristic eschatology in Jesus' message is Marcus Borg's argument that Jesus was a sort of shaman who perceived the kingdom of God "vertically" through mystical experiences (see, e.g., Marcus Borg and N. T. Wright, *The Meaning of Jesus: Two Visions* [San Francisco: HarperSanFrancisco, 1999]).

38. G. R. Beasley-Murray, *Jesus and the Kingdom of God* (Grand Rapids: Eerdmans, 1996).

39. See the discussion in Gerd Theissen and Annette Merz, *The Historical Jesus: A Comprehensive Guide* (Minneapolis: Fortress Press, 1998), 246–64.

40. See Perrin, *Jesus and the Language of the Kingdom* (Philadelphia: Fortress Press, 1976), 16–32. It should be noted that this formulation marked a change in Perrin's understanding of biblical kingdom language, since in his earlier works *The Kingdom of God in the Teaching of Jesus* (Philadelphia: Westminster, 1963) and *Rediscovering the*

Teaching of Jesus (New York: Harper & Row; London: SCM, 1967), he defended an apocalyptic interpretation of the kingdom (as noted by Chilton, *Pure Kingdom*, 10–11). See also W. Emory Elmore, "Linguistic Approaches to the Kingdom: Amos Wilder and Norman Perrin," in Willis, ed., *Kingdom of God*, 53–66.

41. For Perrin's list, see *Language of the Kingdom*, 41–42.

42. Ibid., 43. Here, Perrin is discussing Luke 11:20, but his interpretations of the other kingdom sayings are similarly mythic and existential.

43. Ibid., 48.

44. Ibid., 52–53.

45. Ibid., 54.

46. Chilton, "Introduction," 20.

47. Chilton, *Pure Kingdom*, 32–34.

48. Ibid., 34–35.

49. Ibid., 36–38.

50. Ibid., 38–40; quotation from 39.

51. Ibid., 40–42. On God as king in the Psalms, see *Pure Kingdom*, 146–63.

52. Ibid., 53–54.

53. Ibid., 57–66.

54. Ibid., 66–73.

55. Ibid., 74–80.

56. Ibid. 81–90.

57. Ibid. 90–97.

58. Chilton, "Introduction," 23.

59. As with the previous sections, this discussion is not meant to be an exhaustive survey, but a brief sketch of the relevant contours of the research.

60. S. G. F. Brandon, *Jesus and the Zealots: A Study of the Political Factor in Primitive Christianity* (Manchester: Manchester University Press, 1967); for a survey of earlier Jesus-as-revolutionary hypotheses, see E. Bammel, "The Revolution Theory from Reimarus to Brandon," in *Jesus and the Politics of His Day*, ed. Bammel and C. F. D. Moule (Cambridge: Cambridge University Press, 1984), 11–68.

61. Marcus J. Borg, "Reflections on a Discipline: A North American Perspective," in Chilton and Evans, eds., *Studying the Historical Jesus*, 14–15; an exception is G. W. Buchanan, who placed Jesus and the kingdom of God squarely in the tradition of "Jewish conquest theology" (*Jesus: The King and His Kingdom* [Macon, GA: Mercer University Press, 1984]).

62. E.g., E. P. Sanders, *Jesus and Judaism* (Philadelphia: Fortress Press, 1987); Marcus J. Borg, *Jesus in Contemporary Scholarship* (Valley Forge, PA: Trinity Press International, 1994), 97–126; John Dominic Crossan, *The Historical Jesus: The Life of a Mediterranean Jewish Peasant* (San Francisco: HarperSanFrancisco, 1992), 265–302.

63. Crossan, *Historical Jesus*, 422.

64. Ibid.

65. G. B. Caird, *Jesus and the Jewish Nation* (London: Athlone, 1965); G. R. Beasley-Murray, *Jesus and the Kingdom of God* (Grand Rapids: Eerdmans, 1986); N. T. Wright, *Jesus and the Victory of God* (Christian Origins and the Question of God, vol. 2; Minneapolis: Fortress Press, 1996); Richard A. Horsley, *Jesus and the Spiral of Violence: Popular Jewish Resistance in Roman Palestine* (Minneapolis: Fortress Press, 1993 [1987]); Richard A. Horsley, *Sociology and the Jesus Movement* (New York: Continuum, 1997); Richard A. Horsley and Neil Asher Silberman, *The Message and the Kingdom: How Jesus and Paul Ignited a Revolution and Transformed the Ancient World* (Minneapolis: Fortress Press, 2002); McKnight, *New Vision*. Another scholar who is in substantial agreement with this position is Steven M. Bryan, *Jesus and Israel's Traditions of Judgement and Restoration* (SNTSMS 117; Cambridge: Cambridge University Press, 2002), although he downplays the significance of Jesus' kingdom language for understanding Jesus' position on "Jewish restoration theology" (see 2–3).

66. N. T. Wright, *The New Testament and the People of God* (Christian Origins and the Question of God, vol. 1; Minneapolis: Fortress Press, 1992), 301.

67. See Horsley and Silberman, *Message*, 23–42.

68. Ibid., 54.

69. McKnight, *New Vision*, 118.

70. Ibid., 85, 118. Like Wright (*New Testament*, 268–72), McKnight

holds that Jews of Jesus' time regarded their history of bondage to foreign powers as a continuation of the exile, although the Babylonian captivity had ended in 538 BCE. For a critique of this view, see Bryan, *Jesus*, 12–20.

71. McKnight, *New Vision*, 118; see also 70–117.

72. Ibid., 155; see also 120–54.

73. Rudolf Otto, "The Kingdom of God Expels the Kingdom of Satan," in Chilton, ed., *Kingdom of God*, 31.

74. Mary Rose D'Angelo, "Re-membering Jesus," 199–218; Schüssler Fiorenza, *Jesus and Politics*, 48–51; Jane D. Schaberg, "Magdalene Christianity," in *On the Cutting Edge: The Study of Women in Biblical Worlds*, ed. Jane Schaberg, Alice Bach, and Esther Fuchs (New York: Continuum, 1994), 193–220.

75. Schaberg, "Magdalene Christianity," 197.

76. See, e.g., Judith Plaskow, "Christian Feminism and Anti-Judaism," *Cross Currents* 33 (1978): 306–9; Judith Plaskow, "Anti-Judaism in Feminist Christian Interpretation," in *Searching the Scriptures I: A Feminist Introduction*, ed. Elisabeth Schüssler Fiorenza (New York: Crossroad, 1993), 117–29; Susannah Heschel, "Anti-Judaism in Christian Feminist Theology," *Tikkun* 5:3 (1990): 26–28; Marie Theres Wacker, "Feminist Theology and Anti-Judaism: The State of the Discussion and Context of the Problem in the Federal Republic of Germany," *Journal for the Feminist Study of Religion* 2 (1991): 109–16. See also the discussion in Schüssler Fiorenza, *Jesus and Politics*, 116–23, 153–54.

77. See, e.g., Bernadette J. Brooten, *Women Leaders in the Ancient Synagogue: Inscriptional Evidence and Background Issues* (Brown Judaic Studies 36; Chico, CA: Scholars, 1982); Ross S. Kraemer, *Her Share of the Blessings: Women's Religions among Pagans, Jews and Christians in the Greco-Roman Period* (New York: Oxford University Press, 1992); Amy Jill Levine, "Second Temple Judaism, Jesus and Women: *Yeast of Eden*," in Athalya Brenner (ed.), *Feminist Companion to the Hebrew Bible in the New Testament* (Sheffield: Sheffield Academic, 1996), 302–31; Tal Ilan, "Paul and Pharisee Women," in Schaberg, Bach, and Fuchs, eds., *Cutting Edge*, 82–110; Joan E. Taylor, "The Women 'Priests' of Philo's *De Vita Contemplativa*: Reconstructing the Therapeutae," in Schaberg,

Bach, and Fuchs, eds., *Cutting Edge*, 102–22; Joan E. Taylor, *Jewish Women Philosophers of First-Century Alexandria: Philo's "Therapeutae" Reconsidered* (Oxford: Oxford University Press, 2003).

78. Amy-Jill Levine calls such movements "renewal" or "revitalization" groups ("Women in the Q Communit[ies] and Traditions," in Ross Shepard Kraemer and Mary Rose D'Angleo, ed., *Women and Christian Origins* (New York: Oxford University Press, 1999), 165.

79. D'Angelo, "Re-membering Jesus," 207-8, 209.

80. See, e.g., Schüssler Fiorenza, *Jesus and Politics*, 48–51.

81. Schaberg, "Magdalene Christianity," 197–98.

82. Duling, "Kingdom of God," 64.

83. See Robert W. Funk, *A Credible Jesus: Fragments of a Vision* (Santa Rosa, CA: Polebridge, 2002), 19–28, 133–40.

CHAPTER 5

1. Doron Mendels, *The Rise and Fall of Jewish Nationalism: Jewish and Christian Ethnicity in Ancient Palestine.* (New York: Doubleday, 1982).

2. E.g., Mumford, *Utopias*, 59–60; F. E. Manuel and F. P. Manuel, *Utopian Thought in the Western World* (Cambridge, MA: Belknap, 1979), 46–48; Ferguson, *Utopias* , 146–55.

3. See the discussion in Mendels, *Jewish Nationalism*, 261–75.

4. Jonathan Z. Smith, *Map Is Not Territory: Studies in the History of Religions* (Chicago: University of Chicago Press, 1993 [1978]), 101. Smith contrasts the "locative" worldview with the "utopian," which seeks to transcend limits and boundaries (see 100–103, 130–42, 147–51, 160–66, 169–71, 185–89, 291–94, 308–9). For Smith, the locative worldview is associated with archaic, place-bound modes of thought, whereas the utopian outlook is hellenistic.

5. See Mendels, *Jewish Nationalism*, 273.

6. Doron Mendels, "Hellenistic Utopia and the Essenes," in *Identity, Religion and Historiograpy: Studies in Hellenistic History*, ed. Doran Mendels, (JSPSup 24, Sheffield: Sheffield Academic, 1998), 420–39.

7. R. S. Bluck, "Is Plato's Republic a Theocracy?" *Philosophical Quarterly* 18 (1955): 69.

8. The only surviving writings of Diotogenes are fragments of treatises *On Piety* and *On Kingship* preserved by Joannes Stobaeus (fifth century CE [?], Macedonia). The quoted translation is from Stobaeus 4.7.63, by E. R. Goodenough, "The Political Philosophy of Hellenistic Kingship," *Yale Classical Studies* 1 (1928): 68. For the Greek text, see Johannes Stobaeus, *Ioannis Stobaei Antologium*, ed. C. Wachsmuth and O. Henze (Berolini: Apud Weidmannos, 1884–1912).

9. B. L. Mack, "The Kingdom Sayings in Mark," *Foundations & Facets Forum* 3:1 (1987): 16–17. However, cf. *Pss. Sol.* 17:3; D.C. Duling, "Kingdom of God, Kingdom of Heaven," *ABD*, 4:50–52.

10. *Against Apion* 2.164–65. All quotations of *Against Apion* are from *Josephus: The Life, Against Apion*, ed. H. St. J. Thackeray (LCL 1; Cambridge: Harvard University Press; London: William Heinemann, 1976). Cf. Josephus's statement in *Antiquities* 18.23 that Jews of the "fourth philosophy" held that there should be "no king [*despotēs, hēgemon*] but God."

11. See D. R. Schwartz, "Josephus on the Jewish Constitution and Community," *Scripta Classica Israelica* 7 (1983/1984): 33–34. Josephus's attitude to Jewish monarchy is too complex to discuss in detail here. He elaborates on the Deuteronomistic historian's negative appraisal of the Israelites' wish for a king in the time of Samuel (*Jewish Antiquities* 6.38–44), and paints an unflattering portrait of Aristobulus, the first Hasmonean king (*Jewish Antiquities* 13.301–19). While his portrayals of David and Solomon are generally positive, his source is the Deuteronomistic history, with its ambivalence toward the Israelite monarchy (*Jewish Antiquities* 7.1–8.211). The one king he eulogizes is the ill-fated Saul (*Jewish Antiquities* 6.343–50), for his courage in fighting for his subjects in the face of divinely mandated death.

12. On Josephus's "contemptuous" attitude to the high priests prior to the rebellion, see Seth Schwartz, *Josephus and Judaean Politics* (Columbia Studies in the Classical Tradition 18; Leiden: Brill, 1990), 92–96.

13. S. J. D. Cohen argues that Josephus's prophecy that Vespasian would rule the world constitutes the divine authorization of the Roman victory ("Josephus, Jeremiah, and Polybius," *History and Theory* 21 [1983]: 369–77).

14. Y. Amir, "*Theocratia* as a Concept of Political Philosophy: Josephus' Presentation of Moses' *Politeia*," *Scripta Classica Israelica* 19 (1985/1988): 92.

15. See also the discussions in Duling, "Kingdom of God," 50–52, and Martin Hengel, *The Zealots: Investigations into the Jewish Freedom Movement in the Period from Herod I until 70 A.D.*, trans. David Smith (Edinburgh: T. & T. Clark, 1989), 308–11.

16. See Oscar Cullmann, *The State in the New Testament* (New York: Scribner, 1956), 10–23; Martin Buber, *Kingship of God* (London: George Allen and Unwin, 1967), 136–63; Shemaryahu Talmon, *King, Cult, and Calendar in Ancient Israel: Collected Studies* (Jerusalem: Magnes, 1986); Richard A. Horsley, *Sociology and the Jesus Movement* (New York: Continuum, 1997), 90–96.

17. Talmon, *King, Cult, and Calendar*, 142.

18. See Schwartz, "Josephus," 49–52.

19. All of these sayings were classified as "undoubtedly" (red) or "probably" (pink) authentic by the Jesus Seminar; see Funk, Hoover, and the Jesus Seminar, *The Five Gospels*, 364, 531, 195, 347, 523, 59, 194, 346, 484, 196, 529, 515, 58, 523. The translations used here are from *Five Gospels*, with "kingdom of God/Father's kingdom/kingdom of Heaven" substituted for "God's imperial rule" for the sake of clarity.

20. Especially Mendels, *Jewish Nationalism*, 223–30; Cullmann, *State*, 8–23; see also Geza Vermes, *The Authentic Gospel of Jesus* (Harmondsworth: Penguin, 2003), 401.

21. For an inventory of *basileia* sayings, see John Dominic Crossan, *The Historical Jesus: The Life of a Mediterranean Jewish Peasant* (San Francisco: HarperSanFrancisco, 1992), 457–60. The passages listed in the paragraph above are adduced to make the general point that *hē basileia tou theou/tōn ouranōn* is not identified with Israel in the Jesus tradition; it is not assumed that any or all of them can confidently be attributed to the historical Jesus.

22. See Mendels, *Jewish Nationalism*, 227–29. Luke 22:29-30 (// Matt 19:28) is an exception; it will be argued below that the authenticity of this saying is highly questionable.

23. On Jesus' attitude to the Temple, see Bruce Chilton, *Pure Kingdom: Jesus' Vision of God* (Grand Rapids: Eerdmans, 1996),

115–23; Paula Fredriksen, *Jesus of Nazareth: King of the Jews* (New York: Vintage, 2000), 197–214, 225–32; cf. William R. Herzog, *Jesus, Justice, and the Reign of God: A Ministry of Liberation* (Louisville, KY: Westminster John Knox, 2000), 11–143.

24. Cullman, *State*, 10.

25. Mendels, *Jewish Nationalism*, 229.

26. Ibid.

27. Ibid., 225–28.

28. Ibid., 209–42.

29. Ibid., 214.

30. Ibid., 214–17.

31. Ibid., 216.

32. Ibid., 217.

33. Ibid., 218.

34. Ibid., 219.

35. Ibid., 222.

36. One of the referees for the article on which this chapter is based raised the issue of how the eschatological "son of man" hope fits in with the antipolitical tenor of the kingdom of God argued for here. For the purposes of this book, I am following Crossan's analysis of the Son of Man sayings, which finds that this strand is much less deeply embedded in the Jesus tradition than the kingdom of God material, implying that the historical Jesus did not view himself as the eschatological *huios tou anthrōpou* (son of man/human being) (Crossan, *Historical Jesus*, 454–56).

37. Leela Gandhi, *Postcolonial Theory: A Critical Introduction* (Edinburgh: Edinburgh University Press, 1998), 7.

38. E.g., Crossan, *Historical Jesus*, 265–302; Funk, *A Credible Jesus*, 21–28, 133–39, 147–62. On the opposition between the *basileia* movement and the golden age ideology of the Roman Empire, see Crossan and Reed, *In Search of Paul*.

39. The discussion above does not imply that the question regarding the Messiah's Davidic lineage is anything other than a secondary composition (see Funk et al., *The Five Gospels*, 105). Funk and his coauthors attribute the discussion to "a segment of the Jesus movement in which there was some tension between the messiah as

the son of Adam (a heavenly figure) and the messiah as the son of David (a political, royal figure). Admittedly, there is very little evidence for such tension, but there is even less evidence for such a debate in Jesus' own time" (*Five Gospels*, 105; cf. the debate regarding the Davidic lineage of the Messiah in John 7:42).

40. The parallel in Matt 19:28 is not a *basileia* saying. Funk and his coauthors note that the Lucan verses may have served as the original conclusion to the hypothetical sayings gospel, Q (*Five Gospels*, 389).

41. This is one of the few sayings of Jesus classified as authentic by the Jesus Seminar (Funk et al., *Five Gospels*, 102).

42. Robert W. Funk and the Jesus Seminar, *The Acts of Jesus: The Search for the Authentic Deeds of Jesus* (San Francisco: HarperSan-Francisco, 1998), 71.

43. McKnight, *New Vision*, 85, 126–27.

44. Funk et al., *Acts of Jesus*, 71. Other reasons to doubt the historicity of the Twelve are: the association of the Twelve with the eschatological self-awareness of the early church; all of the Marcan references to the Twelve are redactional; the lists of the Twelve are not consistent among the Gospels (71–72).

45. Funk et al., *Acts of Jesus*, 71.

46. Only the Matthean version has the Twelve sitting on "twelve thrones"; in Luke, the disciples are enthroned and judge the tribes, but they are not explicitly designated as "the twelve."

47. Again, Jesus may well have subscribed to the prophetic notion that divine rule of the world would some day emanate from Zion, as the "temple incident" (Mark 11:15-18 and parallels) implies. For the debate as to the historicity of Jesus' Temple act, see David Seeley, "Jesus' Temple Act," *Catholic Biblical Quarterly* 55 (1993): 263–83; P. M. Casey, "Culture and Historicity: The Cleansing of the Temple," *Catholic Biblical Quarterly* 59 (1997): 306–32; and David Seeley, "Jesus' Temple Act Revisited: A Response to P. M. Casey," *Catholic Biblical Quarterly* 65 (2003): 275–76.

48. On the continuity between John and Jesus, see, e.g., Fredriksen, *Jesus of Nazareth*, 184–97.

49. While the sayings about children are usually interpreted as referring to the innocence, powerlessness, and simplicity of the

young (see, e.g., James Francis, "Children, Childhood," in *Eerdmans Dictionary of the Bible*, ed. David Noel Freedman [Grand Rapids: Eerdmans, 2000], 235), Chilton (*Pure Kingdom*, 83–85) sees the child symbolizing the single-minded pursuit of a desired object: "Making the kingdom one's sole object of interest, the way a child fixes on a toy or a forbidden object, makes one pure enough to enter the kingdom" (84). Another possibility is that the *basileia* movement, like the Pharisaic *havurah*, accepted children as members.

50. The bibliography on this topic is vast; the foundational work is Elisabeth Schüssler Fiorenza, *In Memory of Her: A Feminist Theological Reconstruction of Christian Origins* (New York: Crossroad, 1983).

51. Fredriksen, *Jesus of Nazareth*, 104. Cf. Vermes, *Authentic Gospel*, 406–8.

52. Fredriksen, *Jesus of Nazareth*, 104.

53. Ibid., 108.

54. Ibid.

55. Mendels, *Jewish Nationalism*, 229.

56. The Jesus Seminar attributes these sayings to Mark's concerns about relationships within his own community; however, the reversal theme and the radical social ethos of the sayings bespeak an early stage of the development of the *basileia* movement.

57. The parable of the Good Samaritan (Luke 10:30-35) would also fit this theme; however, contra the Jesus Seminar, the parable is arguably a Lucan composition: it is found only in Luke; the ministry to Samaria is a particularly Lucan interest (Acts 1:8; 8:1, 14, 25; 15:3).

58. See Crossan, *Historical Jesus*, 299–302.

59. See ibid., 261–64; Robert H. Brawley, "Open Table Fellowship: Bane and Blessing for the Historical Jesus," *Perspectives in Religious Studies* 22 (1995): 13–31; McKnight, *New Vision*, 41–49.

60. Cf. Luke 21:18; Matt 7:9-11//Luke 11:11-13; Luke 12:25//Matt 6:27; Matt 7:7-8//Luke 11:9-10//*Gosp. Thom.* 94:1-2; cf. *Gosp. Thom.* 2:1; cf. Luke 10:7-8; *Gosp. Thom.* 14:4; Luke 12:22-23//Matt 6:25; *Gosp. Thom.* 36:1; Luke 12:16-20; *Gosp. Thom.* 63:1-6.

61. Cf. Matt 5:40//Luke 6:29b; Matt 5:41; Matt 18:23-34; Matt 7:3-5//Luke 6:41-42//*Gosp. Thom.* 26:1-2; Matt 6:12//Luke 11:4a-b;

Luke 6:37c//Mark 11:25//Matt 6:14-15; Luke 6:32//Matt 5:46; Matt 5:43-48//Luke 27–28, 32–35. The association of the divine with the sun noted in the Therapeutai, Essenes, and Heliopolitans is found in one saying of Jesus classified as "pink" by the Jesus Seminar. Of course, like the Therapeutai, the children of the *basileia* knew better than to worship the sun; however, in Matt 5:45 the sun is connected with divine providence. The metaphorical association of God with the sun is found frequently in the Psalms (e.g., Pss 19:4; 37:6; 50:1; 72:5; 74:16; 84:11; 136:8; 148:3; cf. Luke 1:78).

62. That the historical Jesus cured some people of their illnesses is accepted even by the skeptical criteria adopted by the Jesus Seminar (see *Acts of Jesus*, 531). The six healing narratives considered by the Seminar to have some claim on historicity are Mark 1:29-31; 1:40-45; 2:1-12; 5:24b-34; 8:22-26; and 10:46-52.

63. See my "Ancient Slavery as an Interpretive Context for the New Testament Servant Parables with Special Reference to the Unjust Steward (Luke 16:1-8)," *Journal of Biblical Literature* 111 (1992): 37–54.

64. On the Essenes as priestly community, see Taylor, "The Women 'Priests,'" 102–22.

Conclusion

1. To paraphrase the much-quoted statement of Rudolf Bultmann, *Theology of the New Testament*, trans. Kendrick Grobel (New York: Scribners, 1951), 33.

2. D'Angelo explains the shift in emphasis from the kingdom to Jesus this way: "Why then to the early churches' memories focus so exclusively around Jesus? One part of that answer is the effect of his death. It was the events of the last week of Jesus' life that made him messiah: it was his death as messiah at the hands of the Romans which affirmed his messiahship in the eyes of his companions" (Mary Rose D'Angelo, "Re-membering Jesus: Women, Prophecy, and Resistance in the Memory of the Early Churches," *Horizons* 19(1992): 213). Jesus, D'Angelo suggests, became iconic to the movement analogously to the elevation of Martin Luther King to iconic status in the African American civil rights movement after his martyrdom. The worship of Jesus after his death is explained by "the early Christian experience

of spirit and prophecy," which enabled his companions to meet him alive after his death (213–14).

3. Karl Paul Donfried, "The Kingdom of God in Paul," in Willis, ed., *The Kingdom of God*, 187.

4. See Mary Ann Beavis, *Mark's Audience: The Literary and Social Setting of Mark 4.11–12* (JSNTSup 33; Sheffield: Sheffield Academic, 1989). See also M. Eugene Boring, "The Kingdom of God in Mark," in Willis, ed., *Kingdom of God*, 131–45.

5. Robert O'Toole, "The Kingdom of God in Luke-Acts," in Willis, ed., *Kingdom of God*, 161.

6. See Robert Hodgson Jr., "The Kingdom of God in the School of St. John," in Willis, ed., *Kingdom of God*, 171–73.

7. Everett Ferguson, "The Kingdom of God in Early Patristic Literature," in Willis, ed., *Kingdom of God*, 200.

8. See Gerd Lüdemann, *Early Christainity according to the Traditions in Acts: A Commentary* (Minneapolis: Fortress, 1989), 61-62.

9. See Dale R. Allison, *The New Moses: A Matthean Typology* (Minneapolis: Fortress Press, 1993).

10. Dennis Duling, "'Egalitarian' Ideology, Leadership, and Factional Conflect within the Matthean Group," *Biblical Theology Bulletin* 27 (1997): 126.

11. Ibid., 131.

12. Ferguson, "Kingdom," 192n2.

13. See Ferguson, "Kingdom"; G. W. H. Lampe, "Some Notes on the Significance of ΒΑΣΙΛΕΙΑ ΤΟΥ ΤΗΕΟΥ, ΒΑΣΙΛΕΙΑ ΧΡΙΣΤΟΥ in the Greek Fathers," *Journal of Theological Studies* 49 (1948): 58–73; John E. Groh, "The Kingdom of God in the History of Christianity: A Bibliographical Survey," *Church History* 43 (1974): 257–67.

14. Alfred Loisy, *The Gospel and the Church* (London: Isbister, 1903), 166.

15. Schaberg, "Magdalene Christianity," 194. Cf. Kathleen E. Corely, "Feminist Myths of Christian Origins," in *Reimagining Christian Origins*, ed. Elizabeth A. Castelli and Hal Taussig (Valley Forge, PA: Trinity Press International, 1996), 49-65; Corley, *Women and the Historical Jesus: Feminist Myths of Christian Origins* (Santa Rosa, CA:

Polebridge, 2002), 7–26; Burton L. Mack, *A Myth of Innocence: Mark and Christian Origins* (Minneapolis: Fortress, 1988).

16. *Apology of Aristides* 16, Syriac version; in *Ante-Nicene Fathers*, ed. Alan Menzies (Peabody, MA: Hendrickson, 1994), 9:276–77.

17. Schaberg, "Magdalene Christianity," 194.

BIBLIOGRAPHY

Albright, W. F. "Primitivism in Ancient Western Asia." In *Primitivism and Related Ideas in Antiquity*, by Arthur O. Lovejoy and George Boas, with supplementary essays by W. F. Albright and P. E. Dumont, 421–32. New York: Octagon, 1935.

Allison, Dale R., Jr. *The New Moses: A Matthean Typology*. Minneapolis: Fortress Press, 1993.

Amir, Y. "*Theocratia* as a Concept of Political Philosophy: Josephus' Presentation of Moses' *Politeia*." *Scripta Classica Israelica* 19 (1985/1988): 83–105.

Anderson, B.W. "Exodus Typology in Second Isaiah." In Israel's Prophetic Heritage: Essays in Honor of James Muilenburg, edited by B. W. Anderson and W. Harrelson, 177–95. New York: Harper & Row, 1962.

Bammel, E. "The Revolution Theory from Reimarus to Brandon." In *Jesus and the Politics of His Day*, edited by E. Bammel and C. F. D. Moule, 11–68. Cambridge: Cambridge University Press, 1984.

Barr, James. *The Garden of Eden and the Hope of Immortality*. Minneapolis: Fortress Press, 1993.

Beasley-Murray, G. R. *Jesus and the Kingdom of God*. Grand Rapids: Eerdmans, 1986.

Beavis, Mary Ann. "Feminist Eutopian Visions of the City," in *Women and Urban Environments 2: Feminist Eutopian Visions of the City*, ed. Mary Ann Beavis, 45–61. Winnipeg: Institute of Urban Studies, 1997.

———. "The Kingdom of God, 'Utopia' and Theocracy." *Journal for the Study of the Historical Jesus* 2 (2004): 91–106.

———. *Mark's Audience: The Literary and Social Setting of Mark 4.11-12*. JSNTSup 33. Sheffield: Sheffield Academic, 1989.

———. "Philo's Therapeutai: Philosopher's Dream or Utopian Construction?" *Journal for the Study of the Pseudepigrapha* 14 (2004): 30–42.

Benko, Stephen. "Some Thoughts on the Fourth Eclogue." *Perspectives in Religious Studies* 2 (1975): 125–45.

Bluck, R. S. "Is Plato's Republic a Theocracy?" *Philosophical Quarterly* 18 (1955): 69–73.

Boccaccini, Gabriel. *Beyond the Essene Hypothesis: The Parting of the Ways between Qumran and Enochic Judaism*. Grand Rapids: Eerdmans, 1998.

Borg, Marcus J. *Jesus in Contemporary Scholarship*. Valley Forge, PA: Trinity Press International, 1994.

———. "Reflections on a Discipline: A North American Perspective." In *Studying the Historical Jesus: Evaluations of the State of Current Research*, edited by B. Chilton and C. A. Evans, 9–31. Leiden: Brill, 1994.

Borg, Marcus J., and N. T. Wright. *The Meaning of Jesus: Two Visions*. San Francisco: HarperSanFrancisco, 1999.

Boring, M. Eugene. "The Kingdom of God in Mark." In *The Kingdom of God in Twentieth-Century Interpretation*, edited by Wendell Willis, 131–45. Peabody, MA: Hendrickson, 1987.

Brandon, S. G. F. *Jesus and the Zealots: A Study of the Political Factor in Primitive Christianity*. Manchester: Manchester University Press, 1967.

Brooten, Bernadette J. *Women Leaders in the Ancient Synagogue: Inscriptional Evidence and Background Issues.* Brown Judaic Studies 36. Chico, CA: Scholars, 1982.

Broshi, M. "Visionary Architecture and Town Planning in the Dead Sea Scrolls." In *Time to Prepare the Way in the Wilderness: Papers on the Dead Sea Scrolls,* edited by D. Dimant and L.H. Schiffman, 9–22. Leiden: Brill, 1995.

Brueggemann, Walter. *The Land: Place as Gift, Promise, and Challenge in Biblical Faith.* Overtures to Biblical Theology. Philadelphia: Fortress Press, 1977.

Bryan, Steven M. *Jesus and Israel's Traditions of Judgement and Restoration.* SNTSMS 117. Cambridge: Cambridge University Press, 2002.

Buber, Martin. *Kingship of God.* London: Allen and Unwin, 1967.

Buchanan, George Wesley. *Jesus, the King, and His Kingdom.* Macon, GA: Mercer University Press, 1984.

Bultmann, Rudolf. *Theology of the New Testament.* Translated by Kendrick Grobel. New York: Scribners, 1951.

Caird, G. B. *Jesus and the Jewish Nation.* London: Athlone, 1965.

Casey, P. M. "Culture and Historicity: The Cleansing of the Temple." *Catholic Biblical Quarterly* 59 (1997): 306–32.

Chilton, Bruce. "The Kingdom of God in Recent Discussion." In *Studying the Historical Jesus: Evaluations of the State of Current Research,* edited by Bruce Chilton and C. A. Evans, 255–80. Leiden: Brill, 1994.

———. *Pure Kingdom: Jesus' Vision of God.* Grand Rapids: Eerdmans, 1996.

———, ed. *The Kingdom of God.* Philadelphia: Fortress Press; London: SPCK, 1984.

Cohen, S. J. D. "Josephus, Jeremiah, and Polybius." *History and Theory* 21 (1983): 366–81.

Collins, John J. "The Jewish Transformation of the Sibylline Oracles." In *Seers, Sibyls and Sages in Hellenistic-Roman Judaism,* 181–98. Leiden: Brill, 1997.

———. "Models of Utopia in the Biblical Tradition." In *A Wise and Discerning Mind: Essays in Honor of Burke O. Long,* edited by

Saul M. Olyan and Robert Culley, 51–67. Brown Judaic Studies 325. Atlanta: Scholars, 2000.

Colson, F. H., and G. H. Whitaker, trans. *Philo*. 10 vols. LCL. Cambridge: Harvard University Press; London: Heinemann, 1985.

Coogan, Michael D., ed. *The New Oxford Annotated Bible, New Revised Version with the Apocrypha*. 3rd ed. Oxford: Oxford University Press, 2001.

Corley, Cathleen E. "Feminist Myths of Christian Origins." In *Reimagining Christian Origins*, edited by Elizabeth A. Castelli and Hal Taussig, 49–65. Valley Forge, PA: Trinity Press International, 1996.

———. *Women and the Historical Jesus: Feminist Myths of Christian Origins*. Santa Rosa, CA: Polebridge, 2002.

Crossan, John Dominic. *The Historical Jesus: The Life of a Mediterranean Jewish Peasant*. San Francisco: HarperSanFrancisco, 1992.

Crossan, John Dominic, and Jonathan H. Reed. *In Search of Paul: How Jesus's Apostle Opposed Rome's Empire with God's Kingdom*. San Francisco: HarperSanFrancisco, 2004.

Cullmann, Oscar. *The State in the New Testament*. New York: Scribner, 1956.

D'Angelo, Mary Rose. "Re-membering Jesus: Women, Prophecy, and Resistance in the Memory of the Early Churches." *Horizons* 19 (1992): 199–218.

Dawson, Doyne. *Cities of the Gods: Communist Utopias in Greek Thought*. New York: Oxford University Press, 1992.

Delumeau, Jean. *History of Paradise: The Garden of Eden in Myth and Tradition*. New York: Continuum, 1995.

Dodd, C. H. *The Parables of the Kingdom*. London: Nisbet, 1935.

Donfriend, Karl Paul. "The Kingdom of God in Paul." In Wendell Willis, ed., *The Kingdom of God in Twentieth-Century Interpretation*. Peabody, MA: Hendrickson, 1987, 175–90.

Duling, Dennis C. "'Egalitarian' Ideology, Leadership, and Factional Conflict within the Matthean Group." *Biblical Theology Bulletin* 27 (1997): 124–37.

———. "Kingdom of God, Kingdom of Heaven." In *ABD*, 4:49–69.

Eisenman, Robert, and Michael Wise. *The Dead Sea Scrolls Uncovered.* New York: Penguin, 1992.

Elmore, W. Emory. "Linguistic Approaches to the Kingdom: Amos Wilder and Norman Perrin." In Willis, ed., *Kingdom of God*, 53–66.

Engberg-Pedersen, Troels. "Philo's *De Vita Contemplativa* as a Philosopher's Dream." *JSJ* 30 (1999): 40–61.

Fairclough, H. Rushton, ed. *Virgil I: Eclogues, Georgics, Aeneid 1–6.* LCL. Rev. ed. Cambridge: Harvard University Press, 1999.

Feldman, Louis H. "Josephus' Portrait of Moses, Part Three." *Jewish Quarterly Review* 83 (1993): 297–328.

Ferguson, Everett. "The Kingdom of God in Early Patristic Literature." In Wendell Willis, ed., *The Kingdom of God in Twentieth-Century Interpretation.* Peabody, MA: Hendrickson, 1987, 191–208.

Ferguson, John. *Utopias of the Classical World.* Aspects of Greek and Roman Life. Ithaca, NY: Cornell University Press, 1975.

Flanagan, James W. "The Deuteronomic Meaning of the Phrase 'kol yiśrā'ēl,'" *Studies in Religion* 6 (1976–77): 159–68.

Francis, James. "Children, Childhood." In *Eerdmans Dictionary of the Bible*, edited by David Noel Freedman, 234–35. Grand Rapids: Eerdmans, 2000.

Fredriksen, Paula. *Jesus of Nazareth: King of the Jews.* New York: Vintage, 2000.

Funk, Robert W. *A Credible Jesus: Fragments of a Vision.* Santa Rosa, CA: Polebridge, 2002.

Funk, Robert W., R. W. Hoover, and the Jesus Seminar. *The Five Gospels: The Search for the Authentic Words of Jesus.* New York: Macmillan, 1993.

Funk, Robert W., and the Jesus Seminar. *The Acts of Jesus: The Search for the Authentic Deeds of Jesus.* San Francisco: HarperSanFrancisco, 1998.

Gandhi, Leela. *Postcolonial Theory: A Critical Introduction.* Edinburgh: Edinburgh University Press, 1998.

Georgi, Dieter. "The Interest in the Life of Jesus Theology as a Paradigm for the Social History of Biblical Criticism." *Harvard Theological Review* 85 (1992): 52–83.

Goodenough, E. R. "The Political Philosophy of Hellenistic Kingship." *Yale Classical Studies* 1 (1928): 55–102.

Groh, John E. "The Kingdom of God in the History of Christianity: A Bibliographical Survey." *Church History* 43 (1974): 257–67.

Hadas, Moses. *Hellenistic Culture: Fusion and Diffusion*. New York: Columbia University Press, 1959.

Haran, Menahem. *Temples and Temple-Service in Ancient Israel*. Oxford: Clarendon, 1978.

Harrisville, Roy A. "In Search of the Meaning of 'The Kingdom of God.'" *Interpretation* 47 (2004): 140–52.

Hengel, Martin. *The Zealots: Investigations into the Jewish Freedom Movement in the Period from Herod I until 70 A.D.* Trans. David Smith. Edinburgh: T. & T. Clark, 1989.

Herzog, William R. *Jesus, Justice, and the Reign of God: A Ministry of Liberation*. Louisville, KY: Westminster John Knox, 2000.

Heschel, Susannah. "Anti-Judaism in Christian Feminist Theology." *Tikkun* 5 (1990): 26–28.

Hodgson, Robert, Jr. "The Kingdom of God in the School of St. John." In Wendell Willis, ed., *The Kingdom of God in Twentieth-Century Interpretation*. Peabody, MA: Hendrickson, 1987, 163–74.

Horsley, Richard A. *Jesus and the Spiral of Violence: Popular Jewish Resistance in Roman Palestine*. Minneapolis: Fortress Press, 1993 (1987).

———. *Sociology and the Jesus Movement*. New York: Continuum, 1997.

Horsley, Richard A., and Neil Asher Silberman. *The Message and the Kingdom: How Jesus and Paul Ignited a Revolution and Transformed the Ancient World*. Minneapolis: Fortress Press, 2004.

Ilan, Tal. "Paul and Pharisee Women." In *On the Cutting Edge: The Study of Women in Biblical Worlds*, edited by Jane Schaberg, Alice Bach, and Esther Fuchs, 82–101. New York: Continuum, 2004.

Janzen, W. "Land." In *ABD* 4:143–54.

Jobling, David. "'Forced Labor': Solomon's Golden Age and the Question of Literary Representation," *Semeia* 54 (1991): 57–76.

Jowett, Benjamin, trans. *Aristotle's Politics*. Oxford: Clarendon, 1920.

Kaiser, Walter C., Jr. "The Promised Land: A Biblical-Historical View." *Bibliotheca Sacra* 138 (1981): 302–12.

Kawashima, Robert S. "The Jubilee Year and the Return of Cosmic Purity." *Catholic Biblical Quarterly* 65 (2005): 370–89.

Kee, H. C., trans. "Testaments of the Twelve Patriarchs." In *The Old Testament Pseudepigrapha* 1, edited by James H. Charlesworth: 775–828. Garden City, NY: Doubleday, 1983.

Klassen, W. "Musonius Rufus, Jesus and Paul: Three First-Century Feminists." In *From Jesus to Paul: Studies in Honour of Francis Wright Beare*, edited by P. Richardson and J. C. Hurd, 85–206. Waterloo, ON: Wilfrid Laurier University Press.

Knauth, Robin J. DeWitt. "Jubilee, Year of." In *Eerdmans Dictionary of the Bible*, edited by David Noel Freedman, 743. Grand Rapids: Eerdmans, 2000.

Knohl, Israel. *The Sanctuary of Silence: The Priestly Torah and the Holiness School*. Minneapolis: Fortress Press, 1995.

Kraemer, Ross S. *Her Share of the Blessings: Women's Religions among Pagans, Jews and Christians in the Greco-Roman Period*. New York: Oxford University Press, 1992.

Kramer, Noah. *Sumerian Mythology: A Study of Spiritual and Literary Achievement in the Third Millennium, B.C.* Philadelphia: University of Pennsylvania Press, 1972.

Kugel, James L. *The Bible As It Was*. Cambridge: Harvard University Press, 1997.

Lampe, G. W. H. "Some Notes on the Significance of ΒΑΣΙΛΕΙΑ ΤΟΥ ΘΕΟΥ, ΒΑΣΙΛΕΙΑ ΧΡΙΣΤΟΥ in the Greek Fathers." *Journal of Theological Studies* 49 (1948): 58–73.

Levine, Amy Jill. "Second Temple Judaism, Jesus and Women: *Yeast of Eden*." In *Feminist Companion to the Hebrew Bible in the New Testament*, edited by Athalya Brenner, 302–31. Sheffield: Sheffield Academic, 1996.

Levine, Etan. "The Land of Milk and Honey." *Journal for the Study of the Old Testament* 87 (2000): 43–57.

Loisy, Alfred. *The Gospel and the Church*. London: Isbister, 1903.

Lüdemann, Gerd. *Early Christianity according to the Traditions in Acts: A Commentary*. Minneapolis: Fortress, 1989.

Mack, B. L. "The Kingdom Sayings in Mark." *Foundations & Facets Forum* 3 (1987): 3–47.

———. *A Myth of Innocence: Mark and Christian Origins*. Minneapolis: Fortress, 1988.

Manning, C. E. "Seneca and the Stoics on the Equality of the Sexes." *Mnemosyne* ser. 4, 26 (1973): 170–77.

Manuel, F. E., and Manuel, F. P. *Utopian Thought in the Western World*. Cambridge, MA: Belknap, 1979.

Marlow, W. Creighton. "Eden." In *Eerdmans Dictionary of the Bible*, 371.

Mays, James Luther. "The Language of the Reign of God." *Interpretation* 47 (2004): 117–26.

McDannell, Colleen, and Bernhard Lange. *Heaven: A History*. New Haven, CT: Yale University Press, 2001.

McKnight, Scot. *A New Vision for Israel: The Teachings of Jesus in National Context*. Grand Rapids: Eerdmans, 1999.

Meier, John P. *A Marginal Jew: Reconsidering the Historical Jesus, Volume 2: Mentor, Message, Miracles*. New York: Doubleday, 1994.

Mendels, Doron. "Hellenistic Utopia and the Essenes." In *Identity, Religion and Historiography: Studies in Hellenistic History*, edited by Doron Mendels, 420–39. JSPSup 24. Sheffield: Sheffield Academic, 1998.

———. *The Rise and Fall of Jewish Nationalism: Jewish and Christian Ethnicity in Ancient Palestine*. New York: Doubleday, 1982.

Menzies, Alan, ed. *Ante-Nicene Fathers*. Vol. 9. Peabody, MA: Hendrickson, 1994.

Millard, A. R. "The Etymology of Eden." *Vetus Testamentum* 34 (1984): 103–5.

Miller, Robert J. *The Jesus Seminar and Its Critics*. Santa Rosa, CA: Polebridge, 1999.

More, Thomas. *Utopia*. Trans. Clarence Miller. New Haven, Conn.: Yale University Press, 2001.

Morris, Paul, and Deborah Morris. *A Walk in the Garden: Biblical, Iconographical and Literary Images of Eden*. Sheffield: Sheffield Academic, 1992.

Mumford, Lewis. *The Story of Utopias*. New York: Boni and Liveright, 1922.

Murphy-O'Connor, J. "La genèse littéraire de la Règle de la Communauté." *Revue Biblique* 76 (1979): 528–49.

Neusner, Jacob. "Qumran and Jerusalem: Two Jewish Roads to Utopia." *Journal of Bible and Religion* 27 (1959): 284–90.

Oppenheimer, Aharon. *The 'Am Ha-aretz: A Study in the Social History of the Jewish People in the Hellenistic-Roman Period*. Trans. I. H. Levine. Leiden: Brill, 1977.

O'Toole, Robert. "The Kingdom of God in Luke-Acts." In Wendell Willis, ed., *The Kingdom of God in Twentieth-Century Interpretation*. Peabody, MA: Hendrickson, 1987, 147–63.

Otto, Rudolf. "The Kingdom of God Expels the Kingdom of Satan." In Chilton, ed., *The Kingdom of God*. Philadelphia: Fortress Press; London: SPCK, 1984, 27–35.

Perrin, Norman. *Jesus and the Language of the Kingdom*. Philadelphia: Fortress Press, 1976.

———. "Jesus and the Language of the Kingdom." In Chilton, ed., *The Kingdom of God*. Philadelphia: Fortress Press; London: SPCK, 1984, 92–106.

———. *The Kingdom of God in the Teaching of Jesus*. Philadelphia: Westminster, 1963.

———. *Rediscovering the Teaching of Jesus*. New York: Harper and Row; London: SCM, 1967.

Perrin, Norman, and Dennis C. Duling. *The New Testament: An Introduction*. 2nd ed. New York: Harcourt Brace Jovanovich, 1982.

Plaskow, Judith. "Anti-Judaism in Feminist Christian Interpretation." In *Searching the Scriptures I: A Feminist Introduction*, edited by Elisabeth Schüssler Fiorenza, 117–29. New York: Crossroad, 1993.

———. "Christian Feminism and Anti-Judaism." *Cross Currents* 33 (1978): 306–9.

Plato. *Republic*. Harmondsworth, Middlesex: Penguin, 1955.

Plaut, W. G. *The Torah: A Modern Commentary*. New York: Union of American Hebrew Congregations, 1981.

Porter, Stanley E. *The Criteria for Authenticity in Historical-Jesus Research: Previous Discussion and New Proposals*. JSNTSup 191. Sheffield: Sheffield Academic, 2000.

Price, Simon, and Emily Kearns, eds. *The Oxford Dictionary of Classical Myth and Religion*. Oxford: Oxford University Press, 2003.

Rawson, Elizabeth. *The Spartan Tradition in European Thought*. Oxford: Clarendon, 1969.

Ringe, Sharon H. *Jesus, Liberation, and the Biblical Jubilee: Images for Ethics and Christology*. Overtures to Biblical Theology. Philadelphia: Fortress Press, 1985.

Romm, James S. *The Edges of the Earth in Ancient Thought: Geography, Exploration, and Fiction*. Princeton, NJ: Princeton University Press, 1992.

Rubinkiewicz, R., trans. "Apocalypse of Abraham." *Pseudepigrapha* 1, 681–705.

Russell, Jeffrey Burton. *A History of Heaven: The Singing Silence*. Princeton, NJ: Princeton University Press, 1997.

Sanders, E. P. *Jesus and Judaism*. Philadelphia: Fortress Press, 1987.

Schaberg, Jane D. "Magdalene Christianity." In *On the Cutting Edge: The Study of Women in Biblical Worlds*, edited by Jane Schaberg, Alice Bach, and Esther Fuchs, 193–220. New York: Continuum, 1994.

Schneekloth, Lynda H. "Unredeemably Utopian: Architecture and Making/Unmaking the World." *Utopian Studies* 9 (1998): 1–25.

Schüssler Fiorenza, Elisabeth. *In Memory of Her: A Feminist Theological Reconstruction of Christian Origins*. New York: Crossroad, 1983.

———. *Jesus and the Politics of Interpretation*. New York: Continuum, 2000.

Schwartz, D. R. "Josephus on the Jewish Constitution and Community." *Scripta Classica Israelica* 7 (1983/1984): 30–52.

Schwartz, Seth. *Josephus and Judaean Politics*. Columbia Studies in the Classical Tradition 18. Leiden: Brill, 1990.

Schweitzer, Albert. *The Quest of the Historical Jesus*. Trans. R. Montgomery. London: Black, 1910.

Seeley, David. "Jesus' Temple Act." *Catholic Biblical Quarterly* 55 (1993): 263–83.

—————. "Jesus' Temple Act Revisited: A Response to P. M. Casey." *Catholic Biblical Quarterly* 65 (2003): 275–76.

Shanks, Hershel. "Searching for Essenes at Ein Gedi, Not Qumran." *Biblical Archaeology Review* (July/August 2002): 90–100.

Smith, Jonathan Z. *Map Is Not Territory: Studies in the History of Religions*. Chicago: University of Chicago Press, 1993 (1978).

Stobaeus, Johannes. *Ioannis Stobaei Antologium*. Edited by C. Wachsmuth and O. Henze. Berolini: Apud Weidmannos, 1884–1912.

Stordalen, T. *Echoes of Eden: Genesis 2–3 and Symbolism of the Eden Garden in Biblical Hebrew Literature*. CBET 25. Leuven: Peeters, 2000.

Stratton, Beverly J. *Out of Eden: Reading, Rhetoric, and Ideology in Genesis 2–3*. Sheffield: Sheffield Academic, 1995.

Sullivan, E. D. S. *The Utopian Vision: Seven Essays on the Quincentennial of Sir Thomas More*. San Diego: San Diego State University Press, 1983.

Talmon, Shemaryahu. *King, Cult, and Calendar in Ancient Israel: Collected Studies*. Jerusalem: Magnes, 1986.

Taylor, J. and P. R. Davies. "The So-Called Therapeutai of 'De vita contemplativa': Identity and Character." *HTR* 91 (1998): 3–24.

Taylor, Joan E. *Jewish Women Philosophers of First-Century Alexandria: Philo's* Therapeutae *Reconsidered*. Oxford: Oxford University Press, 2003.

—————. "The Women 'Priests' of Philo's *De Vita Contemplativa*: Reconstructing the Therapeutae." In *On the Cutting Edge*, 102–22.

Testuz, M. *Les Idées religieuses du livre des Jubilés*. Geneva: Librairie E. Droz, 1960.

Thackeray, H. St. J. *Josephus: The Life, Against Apion*. LCL 1. Cambridge: Harvard University Press; London: Heinemann, 1976.

Thackeray, H. St. J., ed. *Josephus: The Jewish War, Books I–III*. LCL 2. Cambridge: Harvard University Press; London: Heinemann, 1976.

Thucydides. *The History of the Pelopoennesian War*. Trans. Richard Crawley. London: Dent; New York: Dutton, 1945.

Uffenheimer, Binyamin. "Utopia and Reality in Biblical Thought." *Immanuel* 9 (1979): 1–15.

Vermes, Geza. *The Authentic Gospel of Jesus*. Harmondsworth: Penguin, 2003.

———. *The Complete Dead Sea Scrolls in English*. New York: Allen Lane/Penguin, 1997.

Wacker, Marie Theres. "Feminist Theology and Anti-Judaism: The State of the Discussion and Context of the Problem in the Federal Republic of Germany." *Journal for the Feminist Study of Religion* 2 (1991): 109–16.

Waithe, Mary Ellen, ed. *A History of Women Philosophers, Volume 1: 600 B.C.–500 A.D.* Dordrecht: Martinus Nijhoff, 1987.

Wallace, H. N. *The Eden Narrative*. HSM 32. Atlanta: Scholars, 1985.

Weinfeld, M. "Expectations of the Divine Kingdom in Biblical and Postbiblical Literature." In *Eschatology in the Bible and Christian Tradition*, edited by H. Graf Reventlow, 218–31. JSOTSup 243. Sheffield: Sheffield Academic, 1997.

Weisenberg, E. "The Jubilee of Jubilees." *Restoration Quarterly* 3 (1961/1962): 3–40.

Weiss, Johannes. *Jesus' Proclamation of the Kingdom of God*. Trans. H. Hiers and D. L. Holland. Philadelphia: Fortress Press, 1971.

Westermann, Claus. *Genesis 1–11*. Continental Commentaries. Minneapolis: Augsburg, 1984.

Willis, Wendell, ed. *The Kingdom of God in Twentieth-Century Interpretation*. Peabody, MA: Hendrickson, 1987.

Wilson, D. "Iambulus' Islands of the Sun and Hellenistic Literary Utopias." *Science Fiction Studies* 10, no. 3 (November 1976). http://www.depauw.edu/sfs/backissues/10/winston10art.htm.

Wimmer, Joseph F. "Promise." *Eerdmans Dictionary of the Bible*, 1085.

Winiarczyk, M. *Euhemeros von Messene. Leben, Werk und Nachwirkung. Beiträge zur Altertumskunde, Band 157*. Munich: K. G. Saur, 2002.

Wintermute, O. S. "Jubilees." In *The Old Testament Pseudepigrapha*, edited by James H. Charlesworth, 2:35–142. Garden City, NY: Doubleday, 1983.

Wright, Christopher J. H. "Jubilee, Year of." In *ABD* 3:1025–30.

Wright, N. T. *Jesus and the Victory of God*. Christian Origins and the Question of God, vol. 2. Minneapolis: Fortress Press, 1996.

———. *The New Testament and the People of God*. Christian Origins and the Question of God, vol. 1. Minneapolis: Fortress Press, 1992.

Wright, R. B. "Psalms of Solomon." In *The Old Testament Pseudepigrapha* 2, edited by James H. Charlesworth, 667. Garden City, NY: Doubleday, 1983.

INDEX *of* NAMES *and* SUBJECTS

INDEX *of* SCRIPTURE CITATIONS